Santillana Spotlight on English

Academic English for success in content and literacy

STUDENT BOOK 3

Published in the United States of America.

Santillana Spotlight on English
Student Book Level 3
ISBN 13: 978-1-59820-739-2
ISBN 10: 1-59820-739-3

Editorial Staff
Editorial Director: Mario Castro
Developmental Editors: Jill Aronson, Andreina Borges
Design and Production Manager: Mónica R. Candelas Torres
Design and Layout: Francisco Flores Ledesma, Patricia Reyes Ramirez, Nancy Ortega, Erika Gonzales
Image and Photo Research Editor: Monica Delgado de Patrucco
Cover Design and Layout: Studio Montage
Cover Photograph: © Scout Bradley/Getty Images.

Santillana USA Publishing Company, Inc.
2023 NW 84h Avenue, Doral, FL 33122

15 14 13 12 11   3 4 5 6 7 8 9 10

Acknowledgments:
Illustrations: Wally Rodríguez, Marcela Gómez, Cristian Bernardini, Facundo Tello, Emiliano Ordás, Esteban Alfaro, María Wernicke.

Photographs: p.34: © Masterfile, © Robert Sciarrino/Star Ledger/Corbis; p.42: © John Birdsall AGE; p.73: © Francis G. Mayer/Corbis; © Burstein Collection/Corbis; p.76: © Buccina studios AGE fotostock USA; p.89: © Masterfile; p.96: © Lew Robertson/Brand X/Corbis; p.97: © AGE Fotostock USA; p.105: © Bartomeu Amengua AGE Fotostock USA; p.107: © The Gallery Collection/Corbis; p.141: © Mark McMahon; © Franklin McMahon/Corbis; p.170: © Design Pics/Corbis; p.175: © Bettmann/Corbis; © Bettmann/Corbis; p.209: © Brooklyn Museum/Corbis; p.212-213: © Bettmann/Corbis; p.238: © Ramin Talaie/Corbis; p.243: © The Gallery Collection/Corbis; p.244: © Ramin Talaie/Corbis; p.246-247: © Library of Congress Prints and Photographs Division Washington, D.C. 20540 USA; p.250: © Library of Congress Prints and Photographs Division Washington, D.C. 20540 USA; p.251: © Library of Congress Prints and Photographs Division Washington, D.C. 20540 USA; p.252: © Central Pacific Railroad Photographic History Museum; p.253: © Central Pacific Railroad Photographic History Museum; p.254: © Central Pacific Railroad Photographic History Museum; p.255: © Library of Congress Prints and Photographs Division Washington, D.C. 20540 USA; p.257: © Union Pacific Railroad Company; p.256: © Bettmann/Corbis; p.260: © George H. H. Huey/Corbis; p.272: © Hulton-Deutsch Collection/Corbis; p.278: © Bettmann/Corbis.

Table of Contents

Santillana
Spotlight
on English

Unit

1 Back to School

Penny placed her pencils
in her purple pencil case.
Peter paid with pennies
for his picture-perfect paints.
"That's peanuts!" said Penny.
"People pay much more."
"That's pennies!" said Peter.
"Some people are poor."

Topics to explore:

▶ school activities

▶ school locations

▶ school supplies

Spotlight on Reading

Key Words

- buddy
- classroom
- treasure hunt
- playground
- backpack
- eraser
- pencil case
- gym
- cafeteria
- ruler
- main office
- notebook

Predicting

Answer the questions in complete sentences.

1. What does the title of the story tell you?

2. What clues do the key words give you about the story?

3. Where do you think the boy is going?

4. Why do you think his mother is packing his backpack?

5. How do you think the boy feels? Why?

Amir's New School

Written by Susan House

Illustrated by Wally Rodríguez

Today is Monday and it is Amir's first day at his new school. Amir is not happy. He is very upset with his mom.

"I don't want to go to school!" he cries. "I don't have any friends there. I don't know anybody and nobody knows me."

"You have to go to school today," says Amir's mom.

"Okay," says Amir, "but I'm not going tomorrow!"

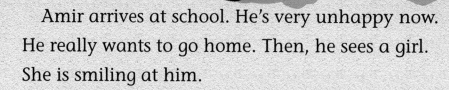

Amir arrives at school. He's very unhappy now.
He really wants to go home. Then, he sees a girl.
She is smiling at him.

"Hi, Amir! My name's Carmen. I'm your buddy,"
says the girl.

Amir is surprised. Carmen knows his name.
Carmen and Amir walk to their classroom together.

Carmen opens the door to their classroom. "This is
Mr. Jackson, our teacher."

"Good morning, Amir!" says Mr. Jackson. Amir is
really surprised that the teacher knows his name!

All the kids shout, "Hi, Amir! Welcome to our class!"
Amir is very surprised now. Everybody knows his name.

Go to a room, just look and look! Find and bring a yellow book.

"I have a surprise," says Mr. Jackson. "Let's have a treasure hunt around the school. Each of you will work with a partner. The first pair to bring me all the objects is the winner."

Carmen and Amir work together.

Carmen and Amir read the first clue.

"I know!" says Carmen. "There are lots of books in the library. We have to find a yellow book in the library. What's the next clue, Amir?"

He reads the next clue.

"Hmm ...," says Carmen, "a place where we can play."

"I know!" says Amir. "The playground! We have to find a red and gray backpack on the playground."

Carmen and Amir solve all their clues. Then, they look for the objects. They find an eraser in the classroom, a pencil case in the gym, a blue pencil in the cafeteria, and a ruler in the main office.

Winners of the treasure hunt.
- First prize: Pencil case and notebook
- Second Prize: Crayons
- Third Prize: Erasers

Mr. Jackson collects all the objects. Then, he announces the winners.

"Listen, everyone, we have our winners!" says Mr. Jackson. "The winners of the treasure hunt are ... Carmen and Amir!"

Mr. Jackson gives them prizes. Amir opens his prize. It is a brand-new pencil case and a notebook.

At three o'clock, it is time to go home. "Good-bye, children! See you tomorrow!" says Mr. Jackson.

Amir's mom is waiting for him.

"This is my buddy, Mom," says Amir. "Her name is Carmen. Bye, Carmen. See you tomorrow."

"But, Amir," says his mom, "you aren't coming to school tomorrow. Don't you remember?"

"Mom, please!" shouts Amir. "Please let me go to school tomorrow. I love school. I have lots of new friends. And everyone knows my name!"

Amir's mom laughs, "That's good! Of course you can go to school tomorrow."

Checking

A Choose the correct answer.

1. This story is about a boy named …
   a. Alex   b. Amir   c. Carmen   d. Mr. Jackson

2. Which sentence is not true?
   a. Carmen and Amir go to the same school.
   b. Carmen and Amir are in the same class.
   c. Carmen and Amir go on a treasure hunt.
   d. Carmen and Amir find only one object.

3. Mr. Jackson gave Amir and Carmen a prize because …
   a. he liked his students.
   b. he was in a new school.
   c. Amir and Carmen found all the objects in different parts of the school.
   d. Amir and Carmen were friends.

4. Why does Amir want to go to school tomorrow?
   a. Amir wants to spend time on the playground.
   b. Amir wants to see Carmen and his other new friends.
   c. Amir wants to make his mother happy.
   d. Amir is afraid of his mother.

B Answer the Critical Thinking questions in complete sentences.

1. Is Carmen someone you would like to have as a friend? Why or why not?

2. Amir was unhappy about going to a new school. Then, he was happy. What caused him to change his mind?

Summarizing

A Fill in the three-column chart to make a Plot graphic organizer.

At the Beginning	In the Middle	At the End
Amir is not happy.		

1. In the first column describe how Amir feels at the beginning of the story.

2. In the second column draw or describe events that happen during the school day.

3. In the third column describe how Amir feels at the end of the story.

B Use the information in your graphic organizer to write a summary of the story. Share your summary with the class.

Reflecting

A Answer the questions in complete sentences.

1. How would you make Amir feel welcome if he was a new student at your school?

2. Carmen said to Amir, "I'm your buddy." What does it mean to be a *buddy*?

B Think about going to a new school. Write sentences to describe things that would make you feel happy or unhappy. Read your sentences to the class.

Spotlight on Language

Connecting

▶ Listen. Use the school map to follow the action.

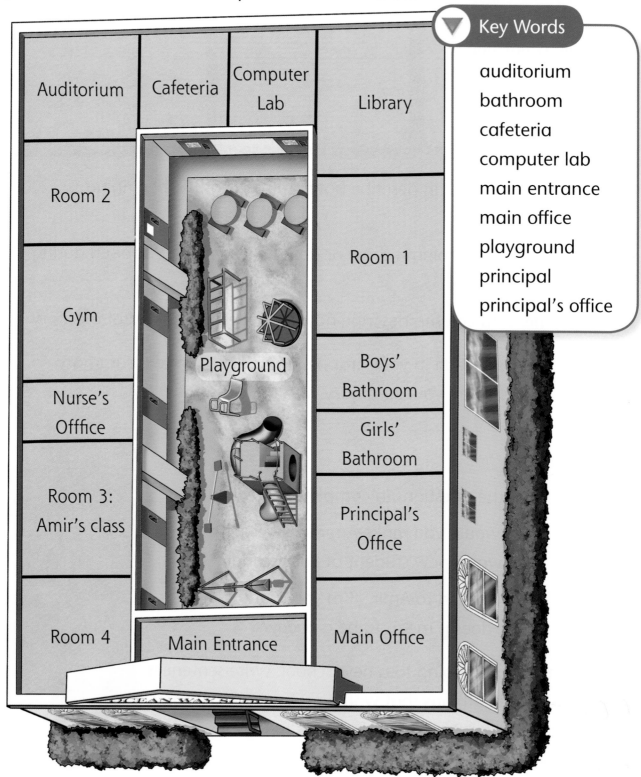

Auditorium

Cafeteria

Computer Lab

Library

Room 2

Room 1

Gym

Playground

Boys' Bathroom

Nurse's Offfice

Girls' Bathroom

Room 3: Amir's class

Principal's Office

Room 4

Main Entrance

Main Office

▼ Key Words

- auditorium
- bathroom
- cafeteria
- computer lab
- main entrance
- main office
- playground
- principal
- principal's office

Focusing

▶ Choose the correct word to complete the sentences according to the school map on page 22.

| in   across   behind   between   next to |

1. Room 1 is _____ from Room 2.

2. Amir's class is _____ Room 3.

3. The nurse's office is _____ the gym and Room 3.

4. The girls' bathroom and the boys' bathroom are _____ each other.

5. The playground is _____ the main entrance.

Applying

A Draw and label a map of your school. Then, write sentences to describe where the following locations are. Use the words *across, behind, between,* and *next to.*

- the principal's office

- the cafeteria

- the nurse's office

B Share your sentences with the rest of the class.

Connecting

A Read and listen to the conversation.

The treasure hunt was fun, Amir. Now let's go meet two of my friends. They are over there.

Hi, Amir! My name is Tino. I hope you like it here. I have been at Ocean Way Elementary School since kindergarten, but I was born in the Dominican Republic.

Hello, Amir. I'm Haruko. I'm from an island called Japan. My name means *spring* in Japanese. I was born in that season, in the month of April.

B Answer the questions in complete sentences.

1. What is a piece of land that is completely surrounded by water called?

2. What is the name for a period of time usually about thirty days? There are twelve of these periods in one year.

3. What is the name for a period of time that is characterized by a particular type of weather?

Focusing

A   Correct any error you may find in the following sentences.

1. Haruko was born in japan.

2. Japan is an Island.

3. Carmen and tino are friends.

4. Haruko was born in the Month of April.

B   Read the following sentences. Circle the specific names of people, places, and things. Then, underline the general words that those words name.

1. Ocean Way is the name of a school.

2. Carmen is Amir's friend.

3. Japanese is a language.

Applying

▶   Create an index card with your personal information.

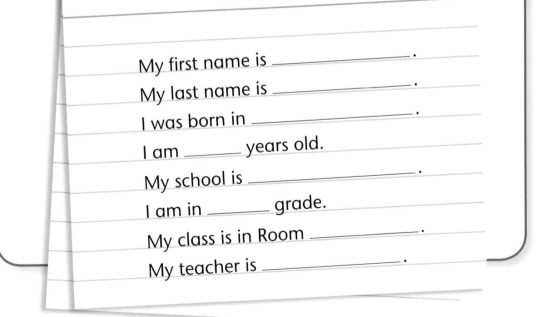

My first name is _____.

My last name is _____.

I was born in _____.

I am _____ years old.

My school is _____.

I am in _____ grade.

My class is in Room _____.

My teacher is _____.

Connecting

A Read what Amir and his friends wrote about their favorite classes.

My favorite class is P.E. Sometimes we play sports. I can throw a basketball or kick a soccer ball. Exercise is important. I want to grow up healthy and strong.

Science is my favorite subject. We can look at really small things with a microscope, like the legs of an ant. We can study really big animals, like an elephant. We find out new things about our world.

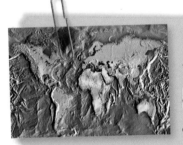

I like social studies. There are so many exciting places in the world. When my grandparents come to visit me, they fly on an airplane. They show me a map of their country. I tell my class all about it.

English is the best class because we get to read fun stories. When you read a book, you go on an adventure. Someday I want to write a book, too.

B Answer the questions in complete sentences.

1. Which is bigger, an elephant or an ant?

2. Is a basketball more like a microscope or a soccer ball? Why?

3. What form of transportation do you use when you fly?

Focusing

▶ Read the questions. Then, complete the answers with the correct word.

a   an

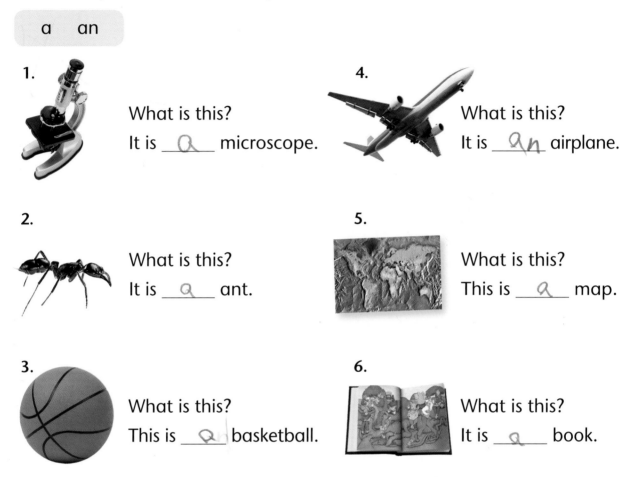

1.

What is this?

It is __a__ microscope.

4.

What is this?

It is __an__ airplane.

2.

What is this?

It is __a__ ant.

5.

What is this?

This is __a__ map.

3.

What is this?

This is __a__ basketball.

6.

What is this?

It is __a__ book.

Applying

▶ Write a paragraph. Describe your favorite class or your favorite sport.

1. Start with a sentence, such as *My favorite class is …*

2. Use the words *a* and *an* in your description. For instance:
   Soccer is an exciting sport.

3. Read the paragraph. Ask yourself: *Will a reader understand this?*
   Make changes you think will help the paragraph to be clearer.

Paragraphs

Northside Elementary School

Northside Elementary School is a great place to go to school. It is for children from kindergarten to fifth grade. There are two classes for each grade. It is called Northside because it is in the northern part of our town.

I have a lot of different friends. Most of them are students at Northside Elementary. My best friend is Marco. He is on my basketball team. His sister Maria is my friend too, but she is in a different grade. My teacher, Mr. Jackson, is also a friend. He watches us on the playground to make sure nobody gets hurt. I like going to school. There I get to see my friends every day.

The school is only three years old. All the rooms are new. There used to be a factory next door, but now it is the playground. It is my favorite place in the school. You can play tag on the field, swing on the swing set, or climb on the monkey bars. I usually play basketball. I am good at shooting baskets. The playground is fun because I get to play with my friends.

▶ Answer the questions in complete sentences.

1. How do you know where a sentence begins and ends?

2. How many sentences are in each group above?

3. How can you tell where a new group of sentences begins?

4. What is the main idea in the second group of sentences?

5. What sentences give details about the main idea in the third group?

Writing Paragraphs

A paragraph is a group of sentences about one main idea. One sentence states the main idea of the paragraph. This is the topic sentence. Often, but not always, the topic sentence is the first sentence in the paragraph. The other sentences give details about the topic sentence.

Tips for writing a paragraph:

- Be sure you begin each sentence with a capital letter.
- Each paragraph should include at least three sentences.
- Be sure to indent the first line of each paragraph.
- Always include a topic sentence in each paragraph.
- Be sure to include details that support the topic sentence.

▶ Write three paragraphs about your school.

1. The first paragraph can be about the location of your school.

2. The second paragraph can be about people in your school.

3. The third paragraph can be about your favorite part of school.

▼ Key Words

details
indent
paragraph
sentence
support
topic sentence

Action Verbs and the Verb *to be*

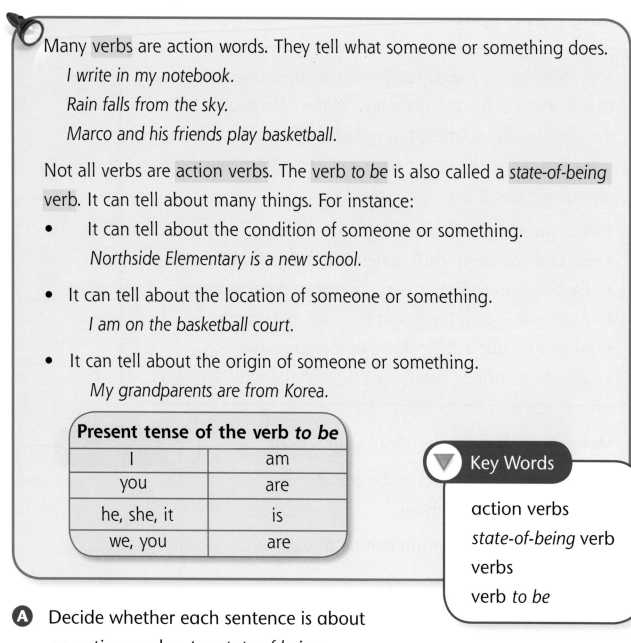

Many verbs are action words. They tell what someone or something does.

I write in my notebook.

Rain falls from the sky.

Marco and his friends play basketball.

Not all verbs are action verbs. The verb *to be* is also called a *state-of-being* verb. It can tell about many things. For instance:

- It can tell about the condition of someone or something.

    Northside Elementary is a new school.

- It can tell about the location of someone or something.

    I am on the basketball court.

- It can tell about the origin of someone or something.

    My grandparents are from Korea.

Present tense of the verb *to be*

I	am
you	are
he, she, it	is
we, you	are

Key Words

action verbs

state-of-being verb

verbs

verb *to be*

A Decide whether each sentence is about an *action* or about a *state of being*.

1. I am a student at Northside Elementary School.

2. Marco plays basketball for his team.

3. My English book is new.

4. Amir visited Pakistan last summer.

5. Mr. Jackson teaches English to third graders.

B Copy and complete each sentence with the correct verb.

1. I ___am___ in third grade. (am/jump)

2. Maria had to ___run___ fast to win the race. (is/run)

3. My dog ___eats___ a lot of food. (is/eats)

4. Learning about science ___is study___ a lot of fun. (is/study)

5. I ___read___ many good books in the library. (are/read)

6. The name of the school ___is___ Northside Elementary. (is/teach)

Revising

A Review the three paragraphs you wrote to complete the activity on page 29.

- Did you use action verbs? Which ones?

- Did you use forms of the verb *to be*? Which ones?

- Are the paragraphs clearly separated?

- Does each paragraph begin with an indented line?

- Does each sentence begin with a capital letter?

B Rewrite your three paragraphs, making any necessary corrections.

Properties of Addition and Subtraction

- An addition is an operation you use to add two or more numbers. The result is the sum.

  Example: 6   +   4   =   10

  six   plus   four   equals   ten.

  10 is the sum.

- A subtraction is an operation you use to subtract two or more numbers. The result is the difference.

  Example: 10   –   4   =   6

  ten   minus   four   equals   six.

  (take away)

  6 is the difference.

- A fact family of addition and subtraction includes four facts, two additions and two subtractions, using the same three numbers.

  Example: 6 + 4 = 10

  4 + 6 = 10

  10 – 6 = 4

  10 – 4 = 6

  The three numbers are 6, 4, and 10.

Key Words

addition
difference
equals
fact family
minus
plus
subtraction
sum

A Read the number sentences aloud.

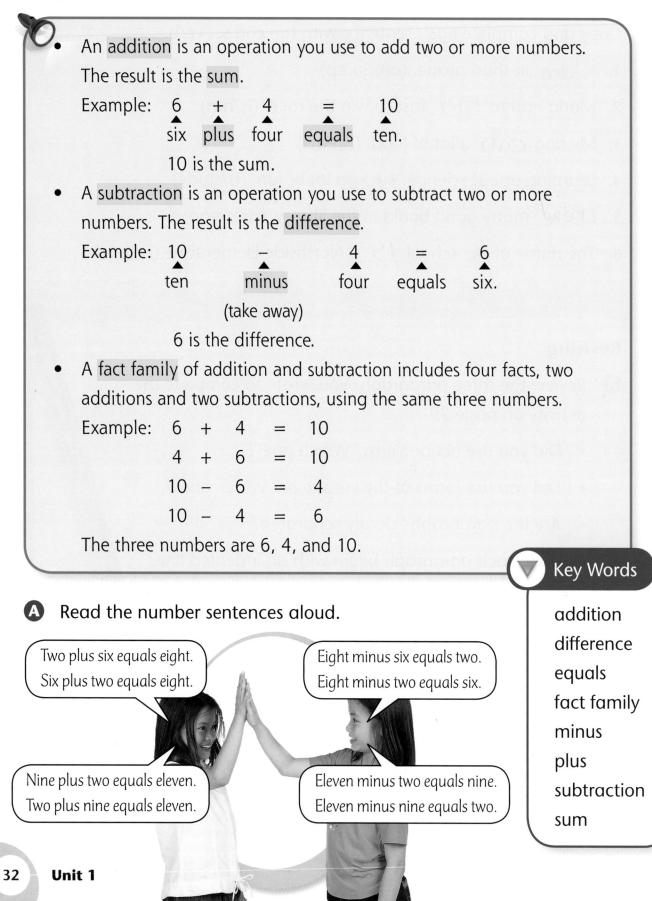

Two plus six equals eight.
Six plus two equals eight.

Eight minus six equals two.
Eight minus two equals six.

Nine plus two equals eleven.
Two plus nine equals eleven.

Eleven minus two equals nine.
Eleven minus nine equals two.

B Complete the following activities.

1. Read the number sentences aloud.

3 + 4 = 7   10 – 8 = 2   7 + 8 = 15   9 – 4 = 5

2. Complete the fact families.

7 + 3 =	10
3 + 7 =	10
10 – 7 =	3

8 + 7 =	15
7 + 8 =	15

3. Write a fact family using these three numbers: 8, 12, 4.

C Solve each problem and answer the questions in complete sentences.

1. Amir borrowed 3 books and 2 DVDs from the school library. Carmen borrowed 2 books and 3 DVDs. What is the sum of the items Amir borrowed? What is the sum of the items Carmen borrowed?

2. Tino bought 16 pencils but gave away 7 to Haruko. What operation do you use to find out how many pencils Tino has left after he gave away 7?

3. What is the name of the result of the operation you use to solve problem number 2?

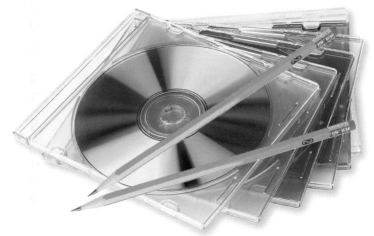

The School Community

A school is a community of students and the people who work at the school. The workers help students learn. They help keep the school safe for everyone. School workers have special jobs to do.

Principal

This person is in charge of running the school.

Teacher

This person is in charge of teaching a class.

Crossing Guard

This person makes sure you cross the street safely.

Food Server

This person makes your lunch and serves it to you.

School Nurse

This person takes care of you when you are sick or hurt.

Custodian

This person is in charge of keeping the school clean and safe.

A Match each worker with the riddle that describes him or her.

1. the teacher

2. the principal

3. the school nurse

4. the crossing guard

5. the food server

6. the custodian

a. I am the person you see if you scrape your knee.

b. I am the person who mops the floor.

c. I am the person who walks you across the street.

d. I am the person who cooks your food.

e. I am the person who checks what you write in your notebook.

f. I am the person who runs the school.

B Write a list of the things your teacher does. Be sure to include a heading or title for your list. Use bullets (•) or numbers to separate items on your list.

C Make a chart of school workers.

1. Draw a two-column chart.

2. In the left column write the names of the school workers you know.

3. In the right column write a sentence that describes what each worker does.

4. Share your chart with the class.

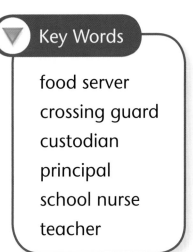

Key Words

food server
crossing guard
custodian
principal
school nurse
teacher

The Scientific Method

The scientific method is a plan that scientists follow. It has five steps.

1. Choose a topic and then ask a question about that topic. For example, the topic would be the boiling point of a liquid, and the question would be *if water boils at 212°F, at what temperature does milk boil?*

2. Form a hypothesis to answer the question. For example, *I think milk will boil at the same temperature as water.*

3. Conduct an experiment to test the hypothesis. For example, to test this hypothesis, you would boil milk in a beaker and measure its temperature.

4. Make and record observations during the experiment. For example, you could watch the milk until it boils, and then use a thermometer to measure and record its temperature.

5. Draw a conclusion based on your observations. For example, you could compare the temperature at which milk boils to the temperature at which water boils.

Magnifying glass: to see an object larger than it is

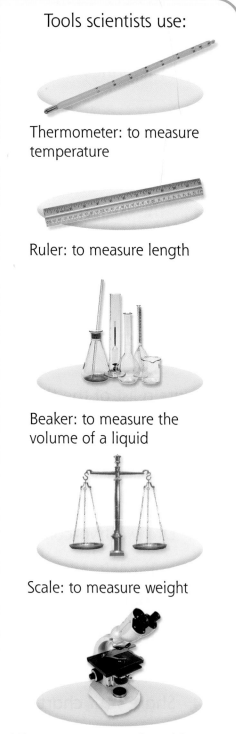

Tools scientists use:

Thermometer: to measure temperature

Ruler: to measure length

Beaker: to measure the volume of a liquid

Scale: to measure weight

Microscope: to see tiny objects very close

A Match each description with the corresponding tool.

1. thermometer

    a. Tino wants to see if his pencil case is heavier than his book.

2. ruler

    b. Carmen is curious about the legs of an ant.

3. beaker

    c. Haruko wants to know the temperature of a pot of water.

4. scale

    d. Amir went to the playground to watch some bugs up close.

5. microscope

    e. Mr. Jackson told the class to measure how tall the board is.

6. magnifying glass

    f. The water cools down, and Haruko wants to know how much water is left.

B Read what the following scientist does. Label each description with the corresponding step of the scientific method shown on page 36.

1. A scientist thinks to herself, "Why do the continents look like jigsaw pieces that fit together?"

2. She uses a computer to measure how the continents could have fit together in the past.

3. She develops an idea that the continents could have begun as one very large mass of land.

4. She tests her idea and finds rocks with the same minerals on several continents.

5. She concludes that her idea was correct.

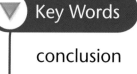

Key Words

conclusion
experiment
hypothesis
observations

Music

Sing Along

A Listen to the song.

The Days Come and Go

Wedne
Th

The days of the week, they come and go,
They come and go, they come and go.

On Monday and Tuesday we go to school,
We read and write, we read and write.

On Wednesday and Thursday we go to school,
We add and subtract, we add and subtract.

Friday comes and we do a review,
We do a review, we do a review.

Saturday comes and Sunday comes,
We play at home, we play at home.

Now the days have come and gone.
It's time to end the song.

B Sing the song.

C What are the days of the week? Which is your favorite
day of the week? Why?

Primary and Secondary Colors

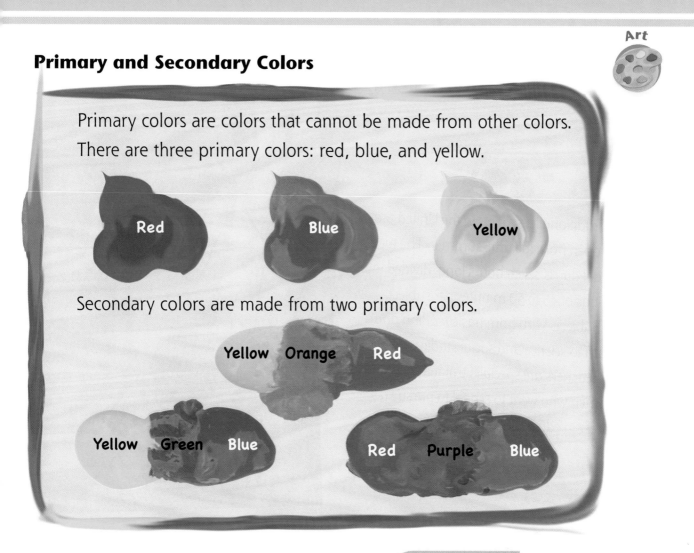

Primary colors are colors that cannot be made from other colors. There are three primary colors: red, blue, and yellow.

Red   Blue   Yellow

Secondary colors are made from two primary colors.

Yellow Orange Red

Yellow Green Blue   Red Purple Blue

A Make color spinners.

1. Color each half of each circle with a different primary color.

2. Push a pencil through the center of the circle.

3. Spin the circles. What colors do you see?

B Write about how many school supplies have primary colors, and how many have secondary colors.

Supplies

- 3 circles made from white poster board, divided in half
- blue, red, and yellow crayons
- pencils

Impressions

United States Schools

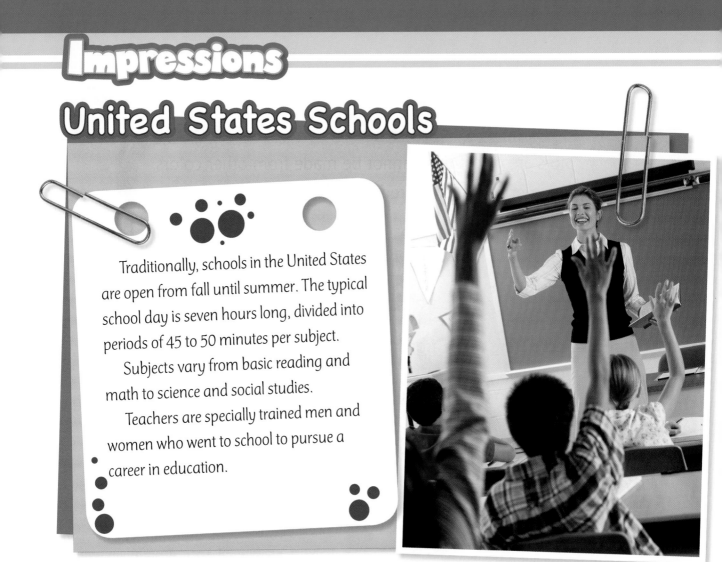

Traditionally, schools in the United States are open from fall until summer. The typical school day is seven hours long, divided into periods of 45 to 50 minutes per subject.

Subjects vary from basic reading and math to science and social studies.

Teachers are specially trained men and women who went to school to pursue a career in education.

A Answer the questions in complete sentences.

1. What is a typical period in the United States classrooms?

2. How is your school similar to or different from the one described in the text?

3. How many subjects do you have?

B Compare your school and the school your parents or your classmates' parents went to.

1. How is it the same?

2. How is it different?

C Fill in a Venn diagram.

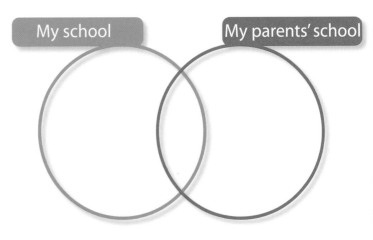

My school

My parents' school

Your Paragraphs

▶ Write three paragraphs about your best friend. He/she is going to attend your school for the first time. Include the following:

- Your best friend's feelings.

- Your plans to make your friend feel more comfortable.

- What you two say when you talk about the school.

- The school supplies your friend might need.

- The subjects your friend prefers.

- Other friends you might want to introduce to your friend.

- The school locations you plan to show to your friend.

The Writing Process

The writing process includes a series of steps:

- **Developing Ideas** Use the Internet, visual elements, or other references to help you gather and develop ideas.

- **Organizing** Choose the ideas you want to use. Put them in order, connect them, or discard the least important ones.

- **Drafting** Use the ideas you organized to write paragraphs.

- **Revising** Read your paragraphs again and correct your writing, keeping in mind what you learned in this unit.

- **Rewriting** Produce a clean copy of your piece, applying all the corrections, to display in class.

You can always repeat a step if you need to.

Unit 2 People Around Me

There is a certain family with both girl and boy children. Each of the boys has the same number of brothers as he has sisters. Each of the girls has twice as many brothers as she has sisters. How many boys and girls are there in that family?

Topics to explore:

▸ people's appearances

▸ clothing

▸ problems and solutions

▸ family members

Spotlight on Reading

Key Words

- picnic table
- sandwich
- braid
- plaid
- freckles
- cat
- shoulders
- lunch bags
- cupcake
- police detective
- bread crumbs
- thief

Predicting

Answer the questions in complete sentences.

1. What does the title tell you the story might be about?

2. What can you tell from the picture about what might happen in the story?

3. What do the key words tell you about what might happen in the story?

The World's Greatest Sandwich

Written by Kathleen Muldoon

Illustrated by A Corazón Abierto

Today our neighborhood is having a block party.
It starts around four o'clock. My mom is working,
so I'm going early because I want to help set up.
The party is in Kim's backyard. She is my best friend.
Some of the other neighbors are also there to help.

I can see Alex and his parents. I can see Ivan and his mother and sister. Elena is sitting under a tree next to her father. He is feeding Elena's baby brother.

"Did you bring your lunch, Timmy?" Kim asks.

"Yes!" I say. "I put my bag on the picnic table."

"I brought the world's greatest sandwich. It has peanut butter, bananas, and tuna fish! YUM!"

Kim has blue glasses and black hair. She wears it in one long braid. She is wearing jeans and a red shirt. I am wearing jeans and a plaid shirt. Kim thinks I look like a farmer with my red hair and freckles. Kim looks at my shirt and laughs. She brushes off some white hairs.

"You have Snowball's hair all over your shirt," Kim says.

"I know," I say. "My cat, Snowball, loves sitting on my shoulders."

"I'm hungry. Are you hungry too?" Kim asks.

"Yes, let's eat!" say Alex and Ivan.

"Good idea! I'm really hungry, too," Elena says.

We all open our lunch bags. I take out a cupcake and some apple juice. Then, I shout.

"Where's my sandwich? Did you take my sandwich, Alex?"

"YUK! NO! I hate tuna fish!" Alex says.

My mother is a police detective. She follows clues and solves robberies. There is a sandwich thief that I need to find. So just like Mom and the other detectives, I start looking for clues. My bag was on the table for one minute. Alex and Ivan were the closest ones to it. But Alex says he hates tuna fish. Maybe Ivan took my sandwich!

"Did you take my sandwich, Ivan?" I ask.

"YUK! NO WAY! I hate bananas!" Ivan replies.

Then, I start to look in the grass. Maybe I can find a good clue there.

"Look! What's that in the grass?" I ask.

"It looks like breadcrumbs!" Kim says. We follow the breadcrumbs to the back door of her house. Elena comes out of the house holding a napkin.

"Did you take my sandwich, Elena?"

"YUK! NO! I hate peanut butter!" Elena replies.

I go back to the picnic table. I want to cry. I'm hungry and I can't find my delicious sandwich.

"Let's think. Who made your lunch?" Kim asks.

"I did. I made it last night."

"Where did you leave the bag?"

I try to remember. First, I made the sandwich. Then, I put it in the bag. After that, I put the bag on the table. Then, I took a cupcake and some juice from the kitchen cabinet.

"Well, I left the bag on the table for a few minutes," I say. "Then, I put it in the refrigerator."

Kim laughs. "I know who has your sandwich. Look in your bag." She points to white hairs in the bottom.

"Snowball! I didn't know she was a thief," I say.

"And I bet you didn't know that she likes peanut butter, banana, and tuna fish sandwiches!" says Kim.

Kim gives me half of her sandwich. She is a great friend and a great detective. After the party, Kim comes to my house. Snowball jumps on my shoulder. She smells like tuna fish, bananas, and peanut butter. She looks very happy.

Checking

A Choose the correct answer.

1. Which character tells the story?

   a. Kim   b. Timmy   c. Elena   d. Alex

2. What does Timmy want to do?

   a. He wants to go to Ivan's house.

   b. He wants to take his cat to the park.

   c. He wants to help prepare for the party.

   d. He wants to wait for his mom to come home.

3. What is Timmy's problem?

   a. He can't find the party.

   b. He can't find his friends.

   c. He can't find his sandwich.

   d. He can't find his cat.

4. Who helps Timmy solve his problem?

   a. Kim   b. Snowball   c. Alex   d. Elena

5. How does Kim know Snowball is the thief?

   a. She smells peanut butter and tuna on Snowball's breath.

   b. She sees Snowball eat the sandwich.

   c. She finds white hairs in the bottom of Timmy's lunch bag.

   d. She sees Snowball run away with Timmy's lunch bag.

B Answer the Critical Thinking questions in complete sentences.

1. Why would Snowball eat Timmy's sandwich?

2. Why does Timmy think Kim is a great friend?

Summarizing

A Fill in the three-column chart to make a Problem and Solution graphic organizer.

Problem → **Attempts** → **Solution**

1. In the first column describe the problem that Timmy had.

2. In the second column describe how Timmy tried to solve the problem.

3. In the third column describe how Kim found the solution.

B Use the information in your graphic organizer to write a summary of the story.

Reflecting

A Answer the questions in complete sentences.

1. What friends do you have in your neighborhood?

2. What would a peanut butter, banana, and tuna fish sandwich taste like?

B Think about the things that you and your friends do together. Write sentences to describe some of those activities. Read your sentences to the class.

Spotlight on Language

Connecting

A Listen to Timmy.

▼ Key Words

blue jeans
he
she
shirt
shorts
skirt
they
T-shirts

B Answer the questions in complete sentences.

1. What is your teacher wearing?

2. What is the boy closest to you wearing?

3. What is the girl closest to you wearing?

Focusing

(A) Choose the correct word to complete the sentences.

> he   she   they   I   you   we   it

1. Timmy is wearing blue jeans. _____ is also wearing a plaid shirt.

2. Kim, Timmy, and Ivan are wearing long pants. _____ are all wearing blue jeans.

3. Elena's clothes are different from the others. _____ is wearing a skirt.

4. Look at yourself. Ask yourself, "What am _____ wearing?"

5. Look at your classmates and yourself. Ask yourself, "What are _____ wearing?"

(B) Answer the questions about the clothes below. Use complete sentences starting with the word *It* or *They*.

1. What color is the cap?

2. What color are the shorts?

3. What color are the sneakers?

4. What color is the sweater?

Applying

▶ Spy on a classmate and write a riddle for the class to guess. Follow the examples:

I spy someone who is wearing a plaid skirt and a pink T-shirt. Who is she?

I spy someone who is wearing blue shorts and black sneakers. Who is he?

Connecting

A Listen and read as Timmy describes his family.

This is my family. My dad is very tall and has short black hair. Look at my mom. She has red hair and freckles, like me. Both my father and mother are strict.

I have an older sister and a younger brother. My sister is serious, but my brother is funny. My sister looks like my dad. She has long black hair, and she is tall also. My brother is only four. He has black hair like my dad and freckles like my mom!

Can you see my grandparents? They are not strict. Grandpa is thin and has a short gray beard. Grandma has curly gray hair and wears big eyeglasses.

B Answer the questions in complete sentences.

1. Is your teacher strict?

2. Do you have long or short hair?

3. How many brothers and sisters do you have? Are they older or younger than you?

Focusing

▶ Choose the correct word to complete the sentences about Timmy's family.

> strict   funny   big   older   red   tall

1. Grandma wears _____ eyeglasses.

2. Grandma and Grandpa are not _____.

3. Timmy's little brother is _____.

4. His mother has _____ hair.

5. Timmy's dad and sister are both _____.

6. Timmy has an _____ sister.

Applying

▶ Draw a picture of yourself or a family member. Write sentences about the person you draw.

1. Some sentences should describe what the person looks like. Use words like *tall* and *thin*.

2. Some sentences should describe how the person acts. Use words like *serious* and *funny*.

I have black hair.
I am tall and funny.
I love to tell jokes.

Connecting

A Read more about Timmy's friends.

Timmy is not the only one who has a pet. His friends have pets, too.

Alex has a black dog named Zoe. Zoe is usually very calm, but sometimes she hears a noise and barks loudly.

Elena has a beautiful aquarium with tropical fish. The fish swim quietly and never stop.

Ivan has a small turtle that lives in the backyard. You have to walk carefully in Ivan's backyard so you don't step on his turtle.

Kim is the only one who doesn't have a pet. But Timmy's cat, Snowflake, often jumps up on Kim's shoulder. Every time it happens, Kim quickly pushes Snowflake off her shoulder.

B Answer the questions in complete senteneces.

1. How often do you answer questions in class?

2. What do you usually do during recess?

3. What do you never do?

Focusing

▶ Complete the sentences with the correct word.

> carefully   never   often   quickly   quietly

1. How _____ do you go to parties with your friends?

2. You should always cross the street _____ .

3. At the library you can sit _____ and read a book.

4. My neighbors have a dog that _____ stops barking.

5. If you scrape your knee at school, go _____ to the nurse's office.

Applying

▶ Write about what things you usually do during a typical school day. Include things that you always do, things that you do sometimes, and things that you never do.

I always arrive at school early. Sometimes I bring my lunch from home, and sometimes I eat the cafeteria food. I never run in the hallway.

Spotlight on Content

Descriptive Writing

My Best Friend

My best friend is Cristina. I like Cristina because she is always smiling. We sit next to each other in class. She has long curly hair, which is very pretty. Her eyes are brown, like mine. Cristina is tall and thin. She is a good runner. When we run together, she leaves me behind.

Cristina and I do a lot of things together. Almost every afternoon, she invites me to her house. Her house is small, but it has a large backyard with tall trees and all kinds of flowers. I like the pink and red roses that have a sweet smell. Sometimes we do our homework sitting in the backyard.

Cristina lets me play with her puppy, Pearl. Pearl's fur is white and soft. Sometimes I hold her in my arms, and sometimes I chase her around the backyard. Both of us like to pet her. Pearl is really pretty. She has big round eyes and a long bushy tail.

▶ Answer the questions in complete sentences.

1. What words describe Cristina?

2. What words describe the backyard?

3. Can you picture in your mind what Pearl looks like? Describe her in your own words.

Writing Descriptively

When you write a description, you use words that tell about the characteristics of something. Depending on your subject, you can write about how it looks, feels, sounds, tastes, and smells. You can describe how it acts. Descriptive writing can be about a person, a place, an animal, an object, or anything else you want to write about.

Descriptive writing should make the reader imagine what you describe.

Tips for writing a description:

- Think of what you are going to write about and picture it in your mind.
- Use your senses to think about how to describe your subject. What you see, hear, touch, smell, and taste are all good things to write about.
- Be sure to use descriptive words when you write. Descriptive words include those that indicate color, size, and shape.

▶ Write a description of a friend or family member who is special to you.

1. The first paragraph should describe what the person is like and what you like about her or him.

2. The second paragraph should describe a place where this person and you go together.

3. The third paragraph should describe something special that this person does for you or that you do for her or him.

Key Words

characteristics
description
descriptive words
imagine
senses

Parts of Speech

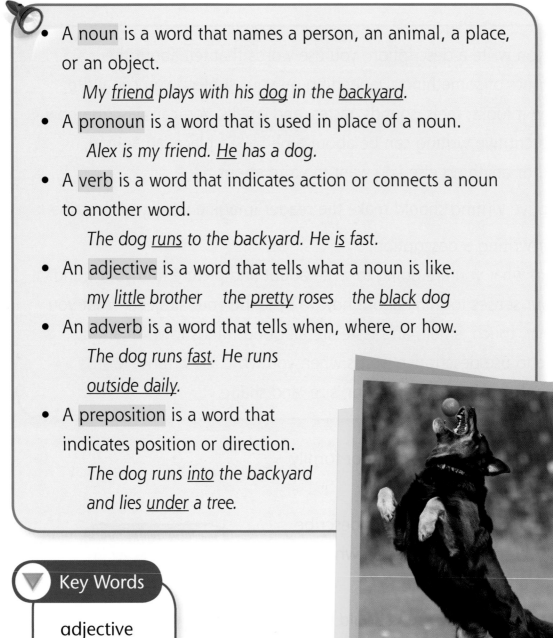

- A noun is a word that names a person, an animal, a place, or an object.

  My friend plays with his dog in the backyard.

- A pronoun is a word that is used in place of a noun.

  Alex is my friend. He has a dog.

- A verb is a word that indicates action or connects a noun to another word.

  The dog runs to the backyard. He is fast.

- An adjective is a word that tells what a noun is like.

  my little brother   the pretty roses   the black dog

- An adverb is a word that tells when, where, or how.

  The dog runs fast. He runs outside daily.

- A preposition is a word that indicates position or direction.

  The dog runs into the backyard and lies under a tree.

▼ Key Words

adjective

adverb

noun

preposition

pronoun

verb

▶ Tell what part of speech each underlined word is.

noun   verb   adjective   adverb   preposition   pronoun

1. The cat is <u>on</u> the table.

2. The backyard is <u>beautiful</u>.

3. I <u>write</u> on the computer.

4. My <u>shirt</u> has a hole in it.

5. <u>She</u> is a funny person.

6. We ride our bicycles <u>carefully</u>.

Revising

Ⓐ Review the three paragraphs you wrote to complete the activity on page 63.

- Did you use adjectives? Which ones describe the special person you wrote about? Which ones describe the place you wrote about?

- Did you use verbs? Which ones tell what the two of you do together?

- Did you write in a way that the reader can picture in his or her mind what you describe?

Ⓑ Rewrite your three paragraphs, making any necessary corrections.

Money

- Money consists of coins and bills. Bills represent dollars, and their values are expressed as a decimal number. These are the most common bills and their values.

$1.00

$10.00

$5.00

$20.00

- Coins represent cents, or parts of one dollar. There are 100 cents in one dollar. Coins have names. Their values are written with the symbol ¢, which means *cents*, or as a decimal number that expresses how much of $1.00 the value of the coin is.

penny = 1¢ or $0.01   **dime =** 10¢ or $0.10

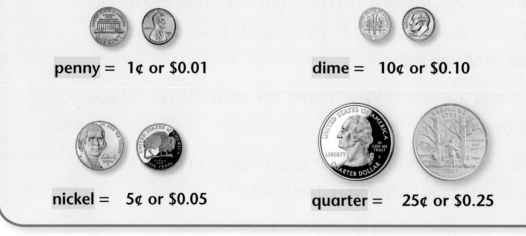

nickel = 5¢ or $0.05   **quarter =** 25¢ or $0.25

BEST CLOTHING SALE!

shorts
$12.95

blue jeans
$20.49

cap
$8.15

T-shirt
$9.20

sneakers
$40.00

sweater
$15.10

▶ Solve the problems and answer the questions.

1. Timmy's parents buy him a sweater for $15.10 and a cap for $8.15. How much do Timmy's parents spend?

2. Kim's parents buy her 2 T-shirts for $9.20 each. How much do Kim's parents spend?

3. You have 2 twenty-dollar bills. Can you buy the $40 dollar pair of sneakers? Will you get change?

4. How much change will you get if you buy the shorts for $12.95 and pay with a ten-dollar bill and a five-dollar bill?

▼ Key Words

bills

cents

coins

dime

dollars

money

nickel

penny

quarter

Family Members

As you probably know, there are names to refer to every member in your family. For example, when you talk to your parents, you call them father and mother, or dad and mom. Your parents call you their son or daughter. If you have siblings, you call them your brother or sister, and they use the same name when they talk about you. What about your grandparents? Who are they? They are your mother's parents or your father's parents. They call you grandson or granddaughter, and you call them grandmother and grandfather, or grandma and grandpa.

What do you call your parents' brothers and sisters? They are your uncles and aunts. They call you their niece or nephew. Their sons and daughters are your cousins. That's easy! It's just one name, whether they are boys or girls.

To make this very simple, there is a graphic way to represent all your family members and their relationships to one another. This is called a family tree. A family tree uses the image of the branches of a tree to show the relationships among members of a family. The members are connected to one another according to how they relate to each other.

▼ Key Words

aunts
cousins
family tree
grandparents
nephew
niece
parents
siblings
uncles

A Look at this family tree.

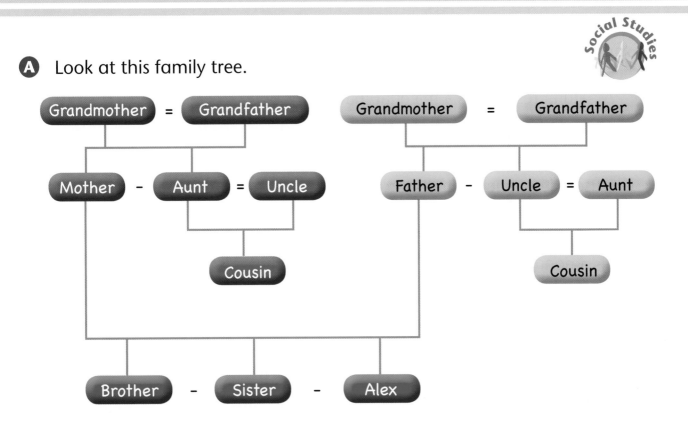

B Explain how each person is related to Alex and to Alex's parents.

C Make a family tree.

1. Write a list of your family members.

2. On a large sheet of paper, draw a family tree like the one in activity A. Fill it in with the members of your family.

3. Below your family tree, write a paragraph that describes relationships among your family members.

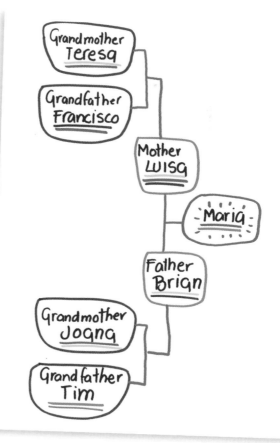

Resources and Conservation

A natural resource is a material that comes directly from nature. There are two types of natural resources, renewable and nonrenewable. Renewable resources replenish themselves over time. They can last forever if they are not overused. Nonrenewable resources cannot be remade or regrown.

Oil is a nonrenewable resource because it cannot be replaced. Oil is formed over many millions of years under the earth's surface. Oil is brought up to the earth's surface and then used to make gasoline, plastics, and other products. Coal and gold are other nonrenewable resources that are taken out of the earth.

Water is an example of a renewable resource. Water is renewable because it is replaced in nature. It falls on the earth as rain, hail, or snow. Trees and wind are other examples of renewable resources.

It is important to conserve natural resources, both renewable and nonrenewable. To conserve something means to use less of it. You can help do this by recycling paper, plastic bottles, and metal cans.

A Match each key word with its definition.

1. renewable

a. use as little as possible

2. nonrenewable

b. cannot be replaced

3. natural resource

c. material from the earth

4. conserve

d. can be replaced

5. recycling

e. reuse of material

B Complete the following activities.

1. Brainstorm a list of natural resources.

2. Underline nonrenewable resources in red and renewable resources in green.

3. Share your list with the class.

C Write about conserving water.

1. Make a list of how people use water every day.

2. Brainstorm ways to use less.

3. Write sentences to tell people how to conserve water.

Key Words

conserve
natural resource
nonrenewable
recycling
renewable

Sing Along

A Listen to the song.

Do Your Ears Hang Low?

Do your ears hang low? Do they wobble to and fro?
Can you tie them in a knot? Can you tie them in a bow?
Can you throw them o'er your shoulder like a Continental Soldier?
Do your ears hang low?

Does your tongue hang down? Does it flop all around?
Can you tie it in a knot? Can you tie it in a bow?
Can you throw it o'er your shoulder like a Continental Soldier?
Does your tongue hang down?

Does your nose hang low? Does it wiggle to and fro?
Can you tie it in a knot? Can you tie it in a bow?
Can you throw it o'er your shoulder like a Continental Soldier?
Does your nose hang low?

Do your eyes pop out? Do they bounce all about?
Can you tie them in a knot? Can you tie them in a bow?
Can you throw them o'er your shoulder like a Continental Soldier?
Do your eyes pop out?

B Sing the song.

C Answer the questions in complete sentences.

1. What do you use your ears for? What do you use your tongue for?

2. What do you use your nose for? What do you use your eyes for?

Pictures of people are called portraits. Some portraits show the whole person. Other portraits show just the person's face. There are many different ways to make paintings of people.

Artists use different kinds of paints and different painting techniques. Some artists' portraits are realistic. They show the person the way he or she looks. Other artists paint in a certain style, interpreting reality in a personal way.

The realistic portrait on the left is a self-portrait.
The portrait on the right is in a style called cubism.

A Draw a self-portrait.

1. Start by lightly drawing the outline of your face, using a pencil. Next, draw your hair, eyes, nose, mouth, and ears.

2. Color in your drawing.

3. When you finish, sign your name below your portrait, the way an artist would do.

B Write a comparison between your self-portrait and the portraits above.

Supplies

- white art paper
- pencil and eraser
- crayons or colored pencils

Impressions

All Kinds of Families

In the United States, we have as many kinds of families as cultures. A traditional family is defined as a basic unit in society usually consisting of two parents and their children. Other family kinds include single-parent families or extended families. The term "extended family" often refers to those people who are related to you but might not live in your home, such as aunts, uncles, cousins, and grandparents.

A Answer the questions in complete sentences.

1. How are families in the United States?

2. What is an extended family?

B Write about the similarities or differences between your classmates' families and your type of family.

Your Descriptive Writing

▶ Write three paragraphs about friends and family members who are special. Include the following:

- Their names and how you know each other.
- What you like about them.
- Things that you share and do together.
- Reasons they are special.

The Writing Process

Remember, the writing process includes a series of steps:

- **Developing Ideas** Use the Internet, visual elements, or other references to help you gather and develop ideas.

- **Organizing** Choose the ideas you want to use. Put them in order, connect them, or discard the least important ones.

- **Drafting** Use the ideas you organized to write paragraphs.

- **Revising** Read your paragraphs again and correct your writing, keeping in mind what you learned in this unit.

- **Rewriting** Produce a clean copy of your piece, applying all the corrections, to display in class.

Remember, you can always repeat a step if you need to.

How many cookies
can a good cookie
cutter cut?
A good cookie
cutter can
cut as many cookies
as a good cookie
cutter can cut.

Topics to explore:

- ▶ daily routines

- ▶ diet and the body

- ▶ the food guide pyramid

- ▶ healthy choices

Spotlight on Reading

Key Words

nutrition

food guide

pyramid

food groups

grain

vegetables

fruit

fat

oil

meat

beans

exercise

lifestyle

Predicting

Answer the questions in complete sentences.

1. What does the title tell you the story might be about?

2. What clues do the key words provide to what the story might be about?

3. Who do you think the story will be about?

The Pyramid of Choices

Written by Andreina Borges

Illustrated by Christian Bernardini

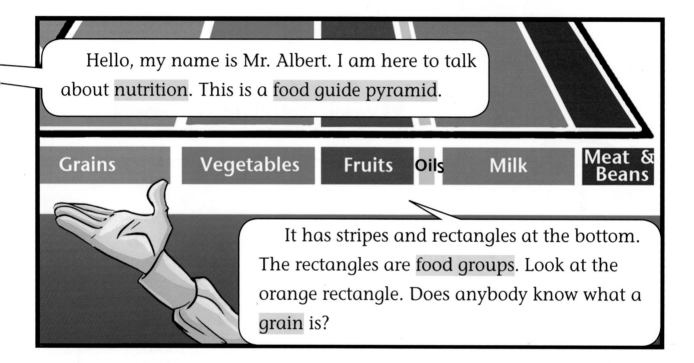

You are absolutely right!

Did you know pasta, bread, and flour are also in this group? If you eat brown rice, whole-wheat bread, and whole-wheat pasta, you will be eating the healthiest grains. Choosing the refined type of these foods will give you fewer nutrients.

What about the stripes?

They have the same color as the food groups. They have different widths. If the stripe is wide, you can eat more of this food group; if it is thin, you should eat less.

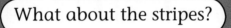

So we can eat more grains than the foods in other groups?

Generally, yes. Now, let's look at the green rectangle.

I know this one. This group is about vegetables, right? I hate veggies.

If you want to have lots of energy, you need to eat broccoli, lettuce, and spinach. They are all green, but did you know that carrots, sweet potatoes, and beets are vegetables? They are very colorful. You can make a fun mix of colors. You should eat them fresh. You can try several to see which one is crunchier. Don't skip your vegetables.

I can see the green stripe is also wide. We have to eat as much of that group as of the grains group, right?

Grains

Vegetables

It all depends on your body's needs. Vegetables have lots of nutrients and fiber that you can use every day. Yes, you should eat lots of them.

What about the red stripe? It is about fruit, right? I like fruit, but only grapes. I hate cantaloupe.

Cantaloupe, bananas, and orange juice have potassium, a mineral that helps our muscles, bones, and heart to stay strong.

You should try them with yogurt or granola. It is important to eat fresh fruit, too. Try different combinations. Never say no to fruit!

Mr. Albert, I see a tiny yellow stripe between the red and the blue one. What is that?

It is not a food group, but your body needs it. That stripe represents oils. Some oils are good because they help the body absorb nutrients from fruits and vegetables. But if you eat lots of oils, they stay in your body and cause health problems. That is why the stripe is so thin: you should only eat a small amount.

Checking

A Choose the correct answer.

1. What does Mr. Albert say about vegetables?
   a. Do not eat vegetables if you do not want to.
   b. Vegetables give you lots of energy.
   c. Never eat vegetables that are crunchy.
   d. Only green foods are vegetables.

2. What does the yellow stripe represent?
   a. bananas
   b. oils
   c. exercise
   d. meat and beans

3. What do the stairs represent?
   a. bananas
   b. oils
   c. exercise
   d. meat and beans

4. How do you know that you should eat more grains and less meat?
   a. The grains stripe is orange.
   b. The grains stripe and the meat stripe are the same size.
   c. The grains stripe is wider than the meat stripe.
   d. The grains stripe comes first.

B Answer the Critical Thinking questions in complete sentences.

1. What is Mr. Albert talking about?

2. How can you tell that students are paying attention to him?

3. What is good nutrition?

Summarizing

A Fill in the Cluster graphic organizer.

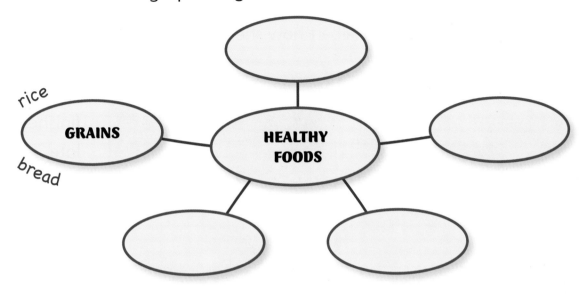

1. Write the names of the food groups inside the bubbles.

2. Write examples of the foods that belong in each group.

B Use the information in your graphic organizer to write a summary. Be sure to include details from the story.

Reflecting

A Answer the questions in complete sentences.

1. What vegetables do you eat?

2. Which food group is your favorite? Why?

3. Why is it important to eat healthy food?

B Make a list of healthy foods to eat for breakfast, lunch, and dinner. Read your list to the class.

Connecting

 A Listen to a student tell Mr. Albert how she exercises.

Key Words

- begins
- early
- finishes
- late
- long
- short
- starts

B Answer the questions in complete sentences.

1. What words do you know that mean the same as *start*?

2. What words do you know that mean the opposite of *short*?

3. How many pairs of opposite words do you know?

Focusing

A Match each word on the left with the word on the right that has the same meaning.

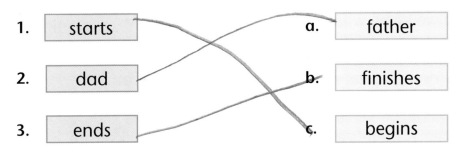

1.	starts		a.	father
2.	dad		b.	finishes
3.	ends		c.	begins

B Match each word on the left with the word on the right that has the opposite meaning.

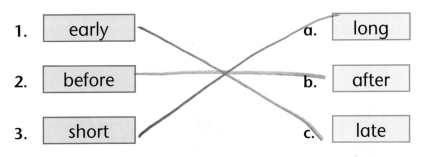

1.	early		a.	long
2.	before		b.	after
3.	short		c.	late

Applying

▶ Write a paragraph about your daily routine.

1. Start with a topic sentence.

2. Add sentences that describe your routine. Use these questions to guide you:

   • What do you do after school, before you eat dinner, and before you go to bed?

   • At what time do you leave for school? At what time do you arrive home?

Most days, I wake up for school at ...

Connecting

A Listen and read as these friends talk about Mr. Albert's visit.

Angela: I'm glad we know what to eat to make us healthy.

Hiro: No more unhealthy food for me!

Angela: I'm only going to eat nutritious foods from now on.

Hiro: Me too! I ate all of my vegetables at dinner last night.

Angela; On weekends there's a farmers' market eight blocks from where I live. I'm going to ask my mom to bring me there to buy lots of healthy snacks.

Hiro: If you pass by my house on your way, I'd like to go with you.

Angela: If we go, it'll probably be at two o'clock, before soccer practice.

Hiro: I'm glad Mr. Albert came here to visit our class. It was good for us to hear him talk. He knows a lot about nutrition.

Angela: Now we know a lot about it, too.

B Answer the questions in complete sentences.

1. What are some examples of things sold at a farmers' market?

2. What is the connection between nutritious foods and healthy people?

3. What are some examples of unhealthy foods?

Focusing

▶ Complete the sentences by choosing the correct word.

1. Hiro _____ all of her vegetables at dinner. (ate/eight)

2. Angela is glad to _____ about healthy foods. (know/no)

3. Hiro should be ready to go with Ling at _____ o'clock. (too/two)

4. Hiro and Ling were happy to _____ Mr. Albert talk to their class. (here/hear)

5. Angela wants her mom to _____ her healthy snacks. (buy/by)

Applying

Ⓐ Make a list of foods that you can try to eat more of and foods you can try to eat less of if you want to have a healthy diet.

Ⓑ Write a paragraph about how a healthy diet can help you be a healthier person. After you have written your paragraph, try to find words in it that sound alike but are spelled differently.

Connecting

A Read the poster that Mr. Albert prepared for the class after his visit.

Healthy Habits

Say YES to

Say NO to

1. Choose Healthy Foods to Eat!

fruits like watermelon and pineapple, and vegetables like carrots and celery

French fries, candies, and chocolate cupcakes all the time

2. Be Active!

playing outdoors

watching television all weekend long

3. Avoid Hazards that cause accidents!

protecting yourself with a helmet and kneepads when you rollerblade

running with untied shoelaces and playing with matches

B Answer the questions in complete sentences.

1. What games do you play outdoors?
2. How do kneepads protect you?

Focusing

A Copy the word in each sentence that is made up of two smaller words.

1. Miguel has a soccer game every weekend.

2. We are in Mr. Jackson's classroom this year.

3. Going outdoors and exercising keeps you healthy.

4. I finished my homework before watching TV.

5. John wrote the answer in his notebook.

B Make new words.

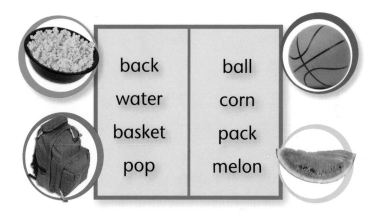

1. Choose a word from the box on the left and a word from the box on the right to make new words.

back	ball
water	corn
basket	pack
pop	melon

2. Use the new words to label the objects.

Applying

▶ Make a chart that lists healthy things you should do and unhealthy things you should try not to do.

1. Label your columns.

2. Use words that are made from smaller words, as much as possible.

Do	Don't
eat whole-wheat pancakes for breakfast	eat cupcakes for breakfast

How-to Article

Melon Smoothies

Ingredients

1 medium-sized cantaloupe
2 tablespoons lemon juice
1 cup vanilla yogurt
1 cup low-fat milk
   sugar to taste

Steps

1. Ask an adult to help you with this recipe.
2. Have an adult cut the melon in half, as you scoop out the cantaloupe seeds with a spoon.
3. Have an adult cut the melon halves into chunks, as you put the melon chunks in a blender.
4. Add the lemon juice, yogurt, milk, and sugar.
5. Have an adult screw the blender jar to the blender, as you turn it on to blend the ingredients until smooth.
6. Serve in glasses with ice cubes.

▶ Answer the questions in complete sentences.

1. How do you know what you will need to make a melon smoothie?

2. How do you know how much of each ingredient to use?

3. Why do you think the sentences are numbered?

Writing a How-to Article

A how-to article tells a reader how to do something. It uses exact words to give directions. What it says has to be accurate and clear. To make the text easier to understand, it is presented as a numbered list of steps. The steps are given in order, from start to finish. Some how-to articles include a list of the things you need to have to make something. A recipe is a type of how-to article.

Tips for writing a how-to article:

- As you write, imagine that you are telling someone how to do something.
- Write each step on a separate line.
- Use verbs that tell the reader exactly what to do.
- If you write a recipe, make sure the quantities or amounts are accurate.

▶ Think of a sandwich you like and write a how-to article that provides directions for assembling it.

1. Write the list of ingredients first.

2. Write the list of steps, and don't forget to number them.

Key Words

article

directions

how-to

list

recipe

steps

Subject-Verb Agreement

The subject of a sentence can be singular or plural. It can be a noun or a pronoun. The verb of a sentence has to agree with the subject. In a sentence with a singular subject, you sometimes add -s or -es to the end of the verb. In a sentence with a plural subject, you do not add -s or -es to the end of the verb.

My sister eats raw vegetables.
They eat raw vegetables.
We wash our hands before we sit down to eat.
She washes her hands before she sits down to eat.

A For each sentence, circle the noun and underline the verb that agrees with it.

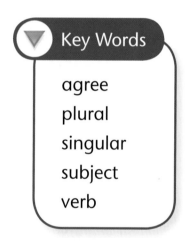

Key Words

agree
plural
singular
subject
verb

1. Jerry eats very quickly.

2. My apple tastes very good.

3. My mother makes melon smoothies.

4. The ice cubes float in the glass.

5. Vegetables taste good with dips and dressings.

B Choose the correct form of the verb to complete each sentence.

1. We always _eat_ salad with dinner. (eat/eats)

2. Some families _goes_ out to eat on Fridays. (go/goes)

3. He _likes_ the smoothies made with yogurt. (like/likes)

4. How many students _attend_ your class? (attend/attends)

5. She _study_ for the quiz. (study/studies)

6. Each color of the food guide pyramid _represent_ a food group.
    (represent/represents)

Revising

Ⓐ Review the how-to article you wrote to complete the activity
on page 97.

- Which verbs are singular?

- Which are the singular subjects that the singular
verbs agree with?

- Is there a list of ingredients for your article?

- Did you write how much to use of each ingredient?

- Are the steps clearly separated and numbered
in sequential order?

Ⓑ Rewrite your how-to article, making any necessary corrections.

Fractions

A fraction is a part of a whole.

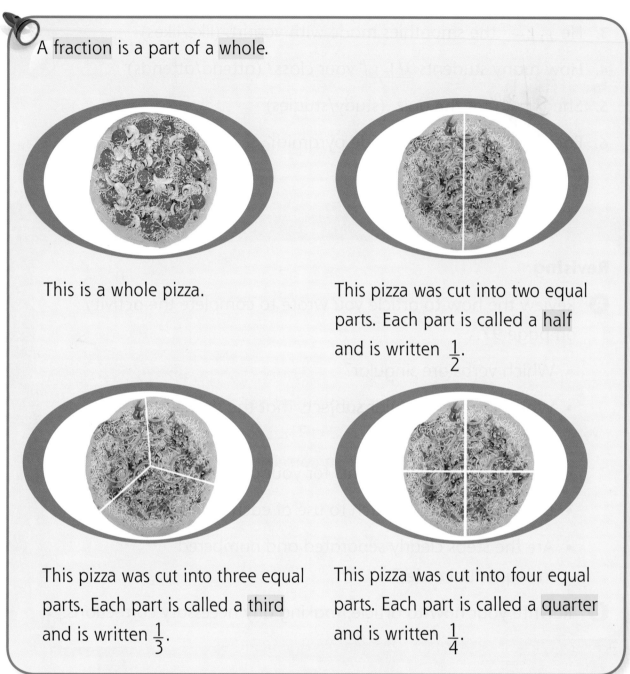

This is a whole pizza.

This pizza was cut into two equal parts. Each part is called a half and is written $\frac{1}{2}$.

This pizza was cut into three equal parts. Each part is called a third and is written $\frac{1}{3}$.

This pizza was cut into four equal parts. Each part is called a quarter and is written $\frac{1}{4}$.

A Match each picture with the fraction that indicates what part of the cake is shown.

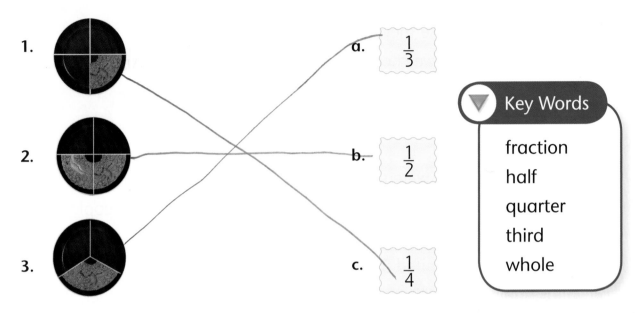

1.

a. $\frac{1}{3}$

2.

b. $\frac{1}{2}$

3.

c. $\frac{1}{4}$

Key Words

fraction
half
quarter
third
whole

B Your mom ordered a large pizza for dinner. A large pizza has nine slices. Your mom ate two slices, your dad ate three slices, your sister ate two slices, and you ate one slice. That left one slice.
Complete the table below with the correct fractions.
Follow the example.

Family Member	Number of Slices	Fraction
mom	2 slices	$\frac{2}{9}$
dad	3 slices	
sister	2 slices	
me	1 slice	
leftover	1 slice	

Imports and Exports

All people need food and water to survive. These are needs because they are things that we cannot live without. If we choose to drink bottled water or flavored water, however, we are moving beyond our need for water into a want for a specific kind of water.

Bottled and flavored waters are goods. Goods are things that can be bought and sold. People buy goods at a grocery store or supermarket. People also sell goods at farmers' markets or flea markets.

Some areas of the United States have better climates or soil conditions for growing certain foods. When one state buys a product from another, it has to transport those goods or send them across the country from one state to another.

Countries also buy and sell goods. If a country has a product, it can sell that product to another country. If a country needs or wants something that it cannot produce enough of or cannot produce at all, that country can buy it from another country. When one country has a supply of goods, that means a quantity of goods or services is being offered for sale at a particular time or at a particular price. When a country sells goods to another country, it exports them or sends them out of the country in exchange for other goods or for money.

When one country has a demand for goods, it has a willingness and ability to purchase goods from another country. When a country buys goods from another country, it imports them, or brings them into the country from someplace else.

Key Words

- demand
- exports
- goods
- imports
- need
- supply
- transport
- want

A Read the chart and answer the questions.

Percentage	Product	State
100%	macadamia nuts	Hawaii
56%	lettuce	California
42%	lettuce	Arizona
68%	oranges	Florida
59%	mushrooms	Pennsylvania
57%	sunflowers	North Dakota

1. If 100% of the macadamia nuts grown in the United States come from Hawaii, what does that mean? What can Hawaii do with all of those goods?

2. If stores in North Dakota need or have a demand for mushrooms, which state are they most likely to get them from? What might they transport to that state in exchange for mushrooms?

3. How much of the supply of lettuce in the United States is grown in both California and Arizona? How much is not grown in either state? What does that mean for the other states?

B The United States' total supply of corn is 13 billion bushels. At least 83% of that corn was grown here. A portion of that corn is exported to other countries. Most of that exported corn goes to Japan and Mexico. Discuss possible reasons why the U.S. would want to export corn to other countries. Then, discuss why Japan and Mexico might want to import corn.

States of Matter

Matter is anything that takes up space. Your body, your books, and the food you eat are examples of matter. Scientists separate matter into three groups according to their state or condition.

▼ Key Words

condition
gas
liquid
matter
shape
solid
state
volume

A liquid has definite volume, but it doesn't have a definite shape. A liquid takes the shape of its container. The water in this glass is a liquid.

A solid has a definite shape and volume. Volume is the space an object takes up. An ice cube is a solid form of water. Liquid water becomes a solid when it freezes.

A gas does not have a definite shape and does not have a definite volume. A gas spreads out. The steam rising from this kettle of boiling water is a gas. Liquid water becomes a gas when it boils.

A Classify each item as a solid, a liquid, or a gas. Then, explain your answers.

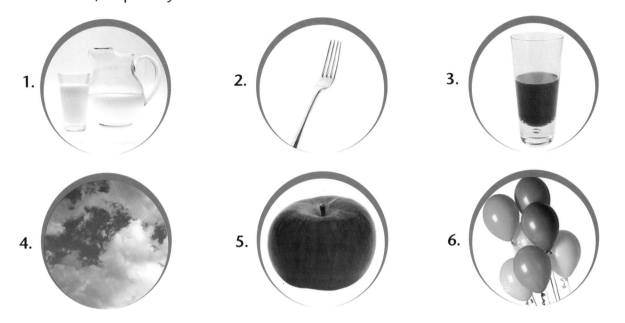

1.

2.

3.

4.

5.

6.

B Answer the questions in complete sentences.

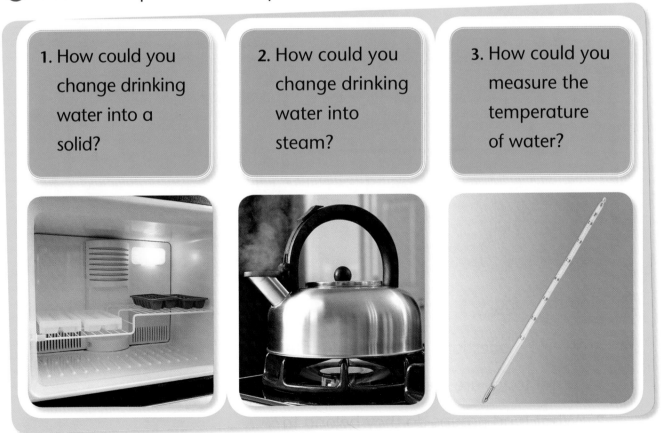

1. How could you change drinking water into a solid?

2. How could you change drinking water into steam?

3. How could you measure the temperature of water?

Sing Along

A Listen to the song.

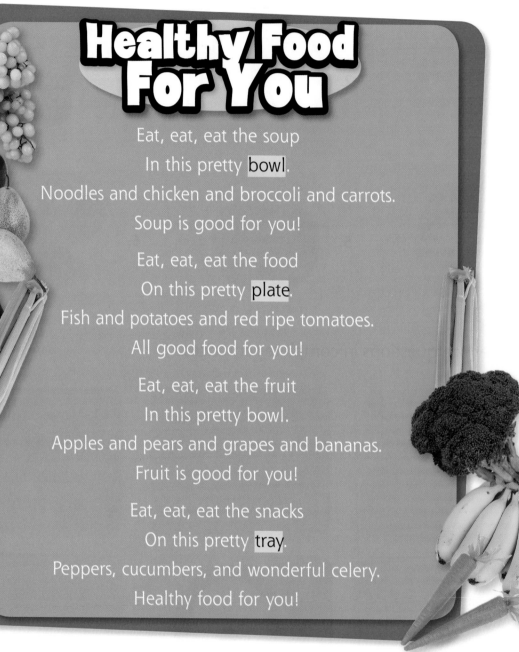

Healthy Food For You

Eat, eat, eat the soup
In this pretty bowl.
Noodles and chicken and broccoli and carrots.
Soup is good for you!

Eat, eat, eat the food
On this pretty plate.
Fish and potatoes and red ripe tomatoes.
All good food for you!

Eat, eat, eat the fruit
In this pretty bowl.
Apples and pears and grapes and bananas.
Fruit is good for you!

Eat, eat, eat the snacks
On this pretty tray.
Peppers, cucumbers, and wonderful celery.
Healthy food for you!

B Sing the song.

C Answer the questions in complete sentences.

1. What foods are mentioned in the song?

2. What food groups do they belong to?

Drawing a Still Life

A still life is a type of painting that shows inanimate objects, or things that do not move. These types of paintings have been popular for hundreds of years. Painters use still life paintings to show many common objects. Flowers, fruits, and vegetables are especially popular. Painters create a display with these objects and then paint what they see when they look at that display.

This example of a still life is by Paul Cézanne, a famous French artist. He uses color to shape the fruits, the white cloth, the basket, and the table. Cézanne's paintings are in museums all over the world.

A Create a still life.

1. On a desk or a table, make an interesting display of classroom objects.

2. Start by drawing the outline of the objects in your display, using a pencil. Next, draw details you see in the objects. Use crayons or colored pencils to fill in your drawing. Try to copy the way that Cézanne used color to shape the objects.

Supplies

- white art paper
- pencil and eraser
- crayons or colored pencils
- classroom objects

B Describe similarities and differences between your still life and Cézanne's.

Impressions

The Horn of Plenty

The Horn of Plenty, or cornucopia, is a symbol of Thanksgiving in the United States. It is typically shown overflowing with the fruits and vegetables of the fall harvest. This abundance of food is what we are supposed to be giving thanks for on that day of celebration. The shape of the horn reflects the horn of a goat, which is also the symbol of abundance in ancient Greek and Roman mythologies.

The fruits and vegetables most often depicted with this symbol include apples, pears, corn, grapes, gourds, pumpkins, and squashes. These are the typical foods harvested in the fall across much of the United States.

A Answer the questions in complete sentences.

1. What is the Horn of Plenty?

2. Why do you think it is important to celebrate the harvest?

3. What does the horn of a goat represent?

B Fold a sheet of paper in thirds lengthwise to form three long columns. In the first column, list your favorite foods from your native country. In the second column, list your favorite American foods. In the third column, list foods from other cultures or countries that you have tried and liked. Include brief descriptions of each dish.

Your How-to Article

▶ Write a four-paragraph essay outlining steps for living a healthy lifestyle. Include the following information in your essay:

- A paragraph that introduces your topic.

- The kinds of foods and activities you need.

- The steps you need to follow to use these foods and activities as part of a healthy lifestyle.

- A paragraph that summarizes and concludes your essay.

The Writing Process

Remember, the writing process includes a series of steps:

- **Developing Ideas** Use the Internet, visual elements, or other references to help you gather and develop ideas.

- **Organizing** Choose the ideas you want to use. Put them in order, connect them, or discard the least important ones.

- **Drafting** Use the ideas you organized to write paragraphs.

- **Revising** Read your paragraphs again and correct your writing, keeping in mind what you learned in this unit.

- **Rewriting** Produce a clean copy of your piece, applying all the corrections, to display in class.

Remember, you can always repeat a step if you need to.

Unit 4 My Community

Many people visit me
every day.
Sometimes they come to
borrow things from me.
Sometimes they come to
return things to me.
I have many volumes, but
I am always silent.
What am I?

Topics to explore:

▶ community locations

▶ community workers

▶ historic buildings

▶ volunteering

Spotlight on Reading

Key Words

train station
theater
library
torn down
history
town hall
mayor
community
local
patrol
traffic
reporter

Predicting

Answer the questions in complete sentences.

1. What does the title tell you the story might be about?

2. Who do you think the people in the picture are? What do you think they will do in the story?

3. What do the key words tell you about what might happen in the story?

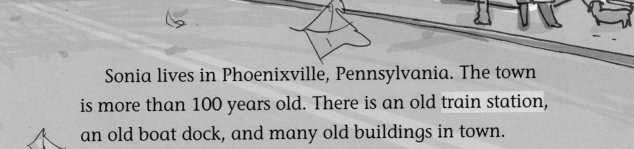

The Show Must Go On!

Written by Betsy Tecco

Illustrated by Facundo Teyo

Sonia lives in Phoenixville, Pennsylvania. The town is more than 100 years old. There is an old train station, an old boat dock, and many old buildings in town.

Sonia loves the Colonial Theater on Bridge Street. She is sad because the owner is closing it. Her mother told her, "It's an old theater and needs a lot of repairs. The owner doesn't have enough money to fix it, so he has to sell it."

Sonia is walking to the library with her mother when they pass the theater. There is a sign on its doors that reads: SAVE ME!

"What does that mean?" Sonia asks.

"It will be torn down if no one fixes it."

"But the theater is so beautiful," says Sonia, "and it's fun to go to the movies there."

"What can we do?" asks her mother.

Sonia thinks and thinks. "Maybe we can find a way to save the theater. There must be something we can do."

Sonia goes to the library. She looks up information about the Colonial Theater. It was built in 1903. Famous people performed on its stage. A very famous magician named The Great Houdini performed there in 1917. In 1958 the theater appeared in a scary movie called *The Blob*. "What a history!" thinks Sonia.

Do Spirits Return?

HOUDINI
SAYS **NO** - AND PROVES IT
3 SHOWS IN ONE
MAGIC · ILLUSIONS · ESCAPES = FRAUD MEDIUMS EXPOSED

THURS. FRI. SAT. SEPT. 2

THEATRE

Then, Sonia and her mother decide to go to the town hall. The mayor works there. They think the mayor can help them save the theater.

"We want to save the theater," Sonia tells him.

"So do we," the mayor replies, "but the theater needs a lot of repairs. The owner doesn't have the money, so he is going to sell it."

"Then, what is going to happen?" asks Sonia.

The mayor frowns. "The theater will be torn down and a new building will be built in its place."

Sonia cries out, "We can't let that happen!"

"People need to show they care about the theater," says the mayor. "If the community believes it is important, it can be saved."

Sonia gets to work. She has a plan! She asks her friends and neighbors to help. Her mother asks local businesses to help. Then, they make signs. The signs read: "The Show Must Go On."

One month later, everyone meets at the theater. Sonia's father arrives in a patrol car with flashing lights. He is a police officer. The police close Bridge Street to traffic. People march up and down carrying the signs. The high school band plays music. Cheerleaders perform. Girls and boys hand out information on the history of the Colonial Theater. The owner of the corner store gives out free bags of popcorn.

Most of the community is there. Sonia has a sheet to sign. The people put their names on a list under the words "Don't Close the Colonial!" They give money to help fix the theater, too. But Sonia wants to do even more.

Just then a newspaper reporter comes by. Her office is behind the theater. "What's going on here?" she asks.

Sonia runs over to the reporter. "We care about the Colonial Theater. We want to keep it open! We have to try and save it."

So the reporter writes a story about Sonia and the theater. The next day, it is on the front page of the newspaper. "The theater is special because it is old," says Sonia in the story. "It is part of our past. If we lose the theater, we lose a part of our history."

Everyone in Phoenixville reads the newspaper story. They agree to save the Colonial Theater. Builders and painters volunteer to fix up the theater. People offer money to pay for new seats. The theater will be more than a movie house. It will become a community arts center. It will be a place for live shows, music, and dance.

Sonia is glad the Colonial Theater is saved. Now she has a new plan. "Someday I will act on the theater's stage!"

Checking

A Choose the correct answer.

1. Why is the owner of the Colonial Theater going to sell it?
   a. He doesn't want to show movies anymore.
   b. He is going to start a new business.
   c. He knows the mayor wants to buy it.
   d. He doesn't have money to repair the building.

2. Why does Sonia want to save the theater?
   a. She wants to save the theater because the owner is her friend.
   b. She wants to save the theater because it is part of the past.
   c. She wants to save the theater because her mother likes the building.
   d. She wants to save the theater because she walks by it every day.

3. Where does Sonia go to look for information about the Colonial Theater?
   a. She goes to the town hall.
   b. She goes to the library.
   c. She goes to the theater.
   d. She goes to the arts center.

4. What happens at the end?
   a. Sonia's plan works, and the Colonial Theater is saved.
   b. The owner gets money to fix the Colonial Theater.
   c. The community decides to tear down the Colonial Theater.
   d. Sonia dances on the stage of the Colonial Theater.

B Answer the Critical Thinking questions in complete sentences.

1. How did Sonia organize her plan and put it into action?

2. What was the result of her actions?

3. Did Sonia's plan benefit the community? Explain your answer.

Summarizing

A Fill in the Sequence graphic organizer.

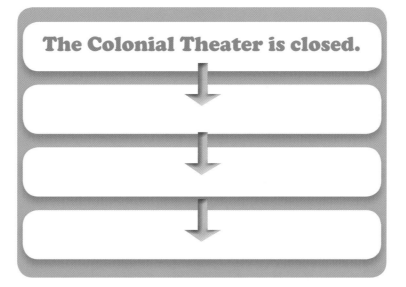

The Colonial Theater is closed.

1. In the first box write what Sonia notices when the story begins.

2. In the second box write what Sonia wants to do.

3. In the third box write how Sonia accomplishes her goal.

4. In the fourth box write what happens at the end of the story.

B Use the information in your graphic organizer to write a summary of the story.

Reflecting

A Answer the questions in complete sentences.

1. How old is the community where you live?
   Does it have historic old buildings?

2. What do old buildings show you about the past?

B Write about your community. Include information such as how old and how big it is, and what you like about it.

Connecting

A   Listen to the conversation.

What's wrong? You don't look happy.

You're right. I'm unhappy. David and I had a plan to go to the Colonial Theater this afternoon. Now, he doesn't want to go.

▼ **Key Words**

disagree
impossible
restart
rethink
unable
unhappy
unusual

B   Answer the questions in complete sentences.

1.   What makes you happy, and what makes you unhappy?

2.   How do you start a computer? How is that different from how to restart a computer?

Focusing

A Choose the correct word to complete the sentences.

1. David doesn't want to go to the Colonial Theater.
   He and Sonia _____. (agree/disagree)

2. Sonia's mother doesn't think that the Colonial Theater is like other theaters. For her the theater is _____. (usual/unusual)

3. Sonia doesn't think that she can do everything. She finds out that some things are _____ for her. (possible/impossible)

4. Sonia is _____ because her cousin David does not want to go to the theater, as planned. (happy/unhappy)

5. Sonia tries to _____ the computer, but she cannot. (start/restart)

6. Sonia's mother thinks it's best for Sonia and David to _____ their weekend plans. (think/rethink)

B Answer the questions in complete sentences.

1. How does the meaning of a word change when you attach *re-* to the beginning of it?

2. How does the meaning of a word change when you attach *un-* to the beginning of it?

Applying

▶ Write about disagreeing.

1. Describe a situation that makes you disagree with someone.

2. When you disagree with someone, describe how you try to make that person agree with you.

I disagree with my mom when she wants me to go to bed early. I want her to rethink my bedtime.

Connecting

A Read and listen.

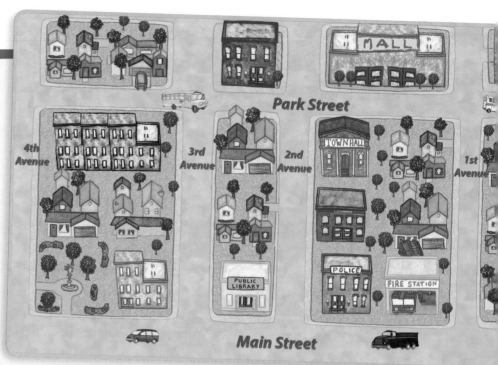

Sonia likes living in Phoenixville because she loves the old historic buildings, like the Colonial Theatre that she helped save. I like living in my community for a different reason.

I live in a community where we can walk to everything. My family lives in an apartment building on Park Street, between Third and Fourth Avenues. From there, I can ride my bicycle to school and to the beautiful park on Fourth Avenue.

When we shop for food, we don't drive anywhere. We walk to the supermarket two blocks away, across from Town Hall. There are also movie theaters and all kinds of stores in the shopping mall where the supermarket is.

The post office is on First Street across from the shopping mall. I go there with my father to mail packages to my grandparents in Honduras.

The public library on Main Street is also very nearby. I go there to borrow books or to use the computer. If I can't find something, the librarian helps me.

I also feel safe in my neighborhood because the fire and police stations are nearby.

B Answer the questions in complete sentences.

1. Where do you live?

2. Where does your family shop?

3. What places are walking distance from your home?

Focusing

▶ Choose the correct word to complete the sentences.

borrow   find   live   love   mail   walk

1. Some people _live_ in apartment buildings.

2. Children and their families _borrow_ books from the public library.

3. The people of Phoenixville _love_ the Colonial Theater.

4. You _find_ things to buy at the mall.

5. At the post office, I can _mail_ a letter to my grandfather.

6. We _walk_ to the supermarket because it's nearby.

Applying

▶ Write about your community.

1. Make a list of places you and your family visit in your community.

2. Write sentences that describe what you do at each place.

-Park
-Library
-Hospital

My family and I have a picnic at the park.

Connecting

A Read Sonia's letter about the rebuilding of the theater.

I want everyone to know that saving the Colonial Theater was a community effort. Many people helped to make it happen.

Both my parents helped. My mother was by my side all the time. My father didn't mind working on weekends to help people know how important it was to save the theater. As a police officer, he knows what it means to be a community worker who works for the people of Phoenixville.

The newspaper reporter who wrote about me also helped. She knows reporting is important for the people of Phoenixville. Everyone who read her report wants to help save the theater.

Then, there is Pablo. He is one of the painters who volunteered to paint the Colonial Theater when it was rebuilt. He spent many hours painting the walls of the building. Pablo works for a builder who builds homes all over Pennsylvania.

B Answer the questions in complete sentences.

1. What does a police officer do?

2. Would the painter work on the theater before or after the builder? Why?

Focusing

▶ Choose the correct word from each group to complete the sentences.

1. **works   worker   working**

   a. Sonia's father _works_ as a police officer.

   b. For him, _working_ for the community is important.

   c. A police officer is a community _worker_

2. **builds   builder   building**

   a. Pablo works for a _builder_

   b. He _builds_ homes in Pennsylvania.

   c. Pablo worked on the _building_ that was saved.

3. **report   reporter   reporting**

   a. This woman works as a _reporter_ for a newspaper.

   b. She is _reporting_ the story of how the theater was saved.

   c. Sonia wrote a _report_ about the history of the building.

Applying

▶ Write questions for a community worker.

1. Think of a community worker whose work interests you.

2. Invite this person to come to your class to talk about the work he or she does.

3. Start your questions with question words.

Where do you work?

What do you like about working here?

Editorials

The New Shopping Mall

Yesterday a group of business people met with the mayor. They presented their plans for building a new shopping mall. The business people want to build a large mall downtown, where our historic buildings are.

Many people in our community don't want to have a new mall downtown. We agree with them. The buildings downtown are part of our history and should not be torn down. A mall can be built anywhere. Putting a new mall downtown would also cause a lot of traffic and make parking very difficult.

Some people in our community don't like malls at all. We disagree with them. Shopping malls provide many jobs to the community. They also let people do all their shopping in one place. Without a mall, people have to drive all over town to buy things.

We are not opposed to shopping malls. We are opposed to tearing down our historic buildings downtown. If a mall is built downtown, what makes our community special will be gone. Is that something we want to do? We don't think so!

Key Words

details

editorial

event

idea

opinion

topic

▶ Answer the questions in complete sentences.

1. Which sentence in the passage describes an opinion?

2. Which sentence in the passage states a fact?

3. How can you determine which statements are facts and which are opinions?

Writing Editorials

An editorial expresses an opinion about a topic, an event, or an idea. The editorial starts by giving information about the topic. It describes the event or idea with exact details so the reader knows what the editorial is about. Then, the editorial goes on to express opinions for or against the topic. The opinions are supported with facts. Editorials are typically found in newspapers.

Tips for writing an editorial:

- Gather reliable information about the topic of your editorial.

- Write down the information for the reader, so that he or she knows the who, what, when, where, why, and how of your topic.

- Make your opinions strong by supporting them with facts. Facts are statements that can be shown to be true.

- Choose words that will persuade the reader to agree with you.

▶ Write an editorial about a current issue.

1. Decide on an issue to write your editorial about.

2. The first paragraph should outline facts related to the issue. The second paragraph should be about what you believe. Support your opinion with facts and persuasive words. The third paragraph should be about the other side of the argument. Use facts to explain why this side is incorrect.

3. Write a conclusion that summarizes your opinion.

Types of Sentences

There are four types of sentences: declarative, interrogative, imperative, and exclamatory.

Declarative

A declarative sentences makes a statement. It says something about a person, an animal, a place, or an object. It ends with a period.

Our neighbors are very friendly.

Phoenixville is a small town in Pennsylvania.

Interrogative

An interrogative sentence asks a question. It ends with a question mark.

How do I get to the Colonial Theater?

Where is my notebook?

Imperative

An imperative sentence asks you to do something. It makes a command or request. It can end with an exclamation point.

You have to stay home today.

John, wait for me!

In some imperative sentences, the subject is understood.

Stop and look both ways before crossing the street.

Go to the library to look up information.

Exclamatory

An exclamatory sentence indicates a strong feeling, and it is said with emotion. It ends with an exclamation point.

Hooray, the theater is saved!

The show must go on!

> **Key Words**
>
> exclamatory
> declarative
> imperative
> interrogative

▶ Determine if each of the following sentences is *declarative, interrogative, imperative,* or *exclamatory.*

1. I really like the park near my house.

2. Where are you going after school?

3. Someone took my sandwich!

4. David, you have to go with me to the theater.

5. There is a lot of history downtown.

6. I love watching movies.

7. Why don't we walk to the library?

8. You have a good plan.

9. Which is your favorite store in the mall?

10. Let's save the theater!

Revising

A Review the editorial you wrote on page 131.

- Did you explain what the issue is?

- Did you explain clearly which side you are on?

- Did you use facts to support your opinions?

- Did you use an exclamatory sentence for emphasis?

- Did you include a conclusion?

B Rewrite your editorial, making any necessary corrections.

Metric Units of Measurement

We use units of length that are standard. In the metric system, the meter is a standard unit of length. Other metric units are derived from the meter in multiples of ten.

$$1 \text{ meter (m)} = 10 \text{ decimeters (dm)}$$

$$1 \text{ meter (m)} = 100 \text{ centimeters (cm)}$$

$$1 \text{ meter (m)} = 1{,}000 \text{ millimeters (mm)}$$

Notice how the names of the units related to the meter begin with a prefix that is attached to the word *meter*. The prefixes have specific meanings:

deci- = tenth

centi- = hundredth

milli- = thousandth

A Compare the measurements.

1. If an object is 5 centimeters wide, and another is 5 millimeters wide, which is wider?

2. If an object is 10 millimeters long, and another is 2 centimeters long, which is longer?

3. If an object's height measures 85 centimeters, and another object's height measures 2 meters, which is taller?

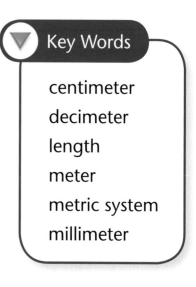

Key Words

centimeter

decimeter

length

meter

metric system

millimeter

B Look at a metric ruler. Identify a millimeter and a centimeter on the ruler. Then, answer the questions.

1. Would you use meters, centimeters, or millimeters to measure the length of a paper clip?

2. Would you use meters, centimeters, or millimeters to measure the height of a person?

3. Would you use meters, centimeters, or millimeters to measure the width of a table?

C A liter is a unit of measure for liquids. A gram is a unit of measure for weight. Use the prefixes you have learned to answer the questions.

1. If one bottle of liquid soap holds 5 centiliters, and another bottle of liquid soap holds 5 milliliters, which bottle holds more liquid soap?

2. If one object weighs 10 milligrams, and another weighs 2 centigrams, which is heavier?

3. If one bucket holds 15 centiliters of water, and another bucket holds 35 milliliters of water, which bucket is holding more water?

4. If one object weighs 100 milligrams, and another weighs 10 centigrams, which object is heavier?

Federal Government

The federal government is the central government of the entire country. It has three branches, or sections. The location of the federal government is Washington DC, the capital of the United States.

The executive branch consists of the president and his or her cabinet, or the people who work with the president in the White House. The president is the leader of the country. Together with the cabinet, the president makes sure that the laws are obeyed.

The legislative branch consists of Congress and its members. Congress is divided into two sections: the Senate and the House of Representatives. Members of Congress represent their states. Congress is in charge of making laws.

The judicial branch consists of the courts and its judges. Courts decide arguments about the meaning of laws to make sure that they are applied in a fair way. The highest court in the country is the Supreme Court.

Key Words

branch
cabinet
capital
executive
federal government
judicial
legislative
president

A Match each definition with the corresponding term.

1. branch of government in charge of enforcing laws

2. home of the president

3. branch of government that includes the Supreme Court

4. leader of the country

5. branch of government in charge of making laws

a. president

b. judicial branch

c. executive branch

d. legislative branch

e. White House

B Complete the sentences.

1. The current president of the United States is _____.

2. The two sections of Congress are called the _____ and the _____.

3. The Supreme Court decides arguments about _____.

4. The vice president is a member of the president's _____.

C Write about the branches of government.

1. Why do you think the federal government is divided into three branches?

2. How do you think state and local governments might be organized?

Earth Materials

Earth materials are solid rocks and soils, water, and the gases that make up the atmosphere. These materials have different physical and chemical properties that make them useful in different ways. Earth materials provide many of the resources that humans use. For example, rocks can be used as building materials; gases and oils found under the ground can be used as sources of fuel; and soils can be used for growing the plants we use as food.

Rocks vary in size, from tiny pebbles to huge mountains. They also vary in shape, color, and texture. Size, shape, color, and texture are known as properties of rocks. Some rocks are made of a single material, but most are made of several materials. These substances are called minerals. Minerals are substances that we find in nature, but are neither plants nor animals.

Soils have properties of color and texture. They can hold water, and they can support the growth of many kinds of plants, including those in our food supply.

A Take a walk around the school playground, a park, or your neighborhood. Observe the ground. What is the difference between the street, the sidewalk, and the soil? What are they made of? What color are they?

B Find a rock in the school playground, a park, or your neighborhood.

1. Observe the rock using all of your senses:
   a. What does it feel like? Is it sharp or smooth?
   b. How heavy is it? Does it feel heavy or light?
   c. What does it look like? Does it sparkle or is it dull?
   d. Is it all one color, or does it have different colors?
   e. What does it smell like? Does it have an odor?

2. Observe the rock using a magnifying glass. Do you notice anything else about the rock that you did not see before? Describe what you observe.

C Write about the rock.

1. Describe where you found the rock. Be sure to include details about the soil you found it in and what was near it.

2. Describe what you observed about the rock.

3. Describe where you think the rock might have come from.

Key Words

minerals
properties
resources
rocks
soils

Sing Along

A Listen to the song.

If I Had a Hammer(*)

If I had a hammer, I'd hammer in the morning,
I'd hammer in the evening, all over this land.
I'd hammer out danger, I'd hammer out a warning,
I'd hammer out love between my brothers and my sisters
All over this land.

If I had a bell, I'd ring it in the morning,
I'd ring it in the evening, all over this land.
I'd ring out danger, I'd ring out a warning,
I'd ring out love between my brothers and my sisters
All over this land.

If I had a song, I'd sing it in the morning,
I'd sing it in the evening, all over this land.
I'd sing out danger, I'd sing out a warning,
I'd sing out love between my brothers and my sisters
All over this land.

Well I've got a hammer, and I've got a bell,
And I've got a song to sing, all over this land.

It's the hammer of justice, it's the bell of freedom,
It's the song about love between my brothers and my sisters
All over this land.

(*) by Pete Seeger and Lee Hays

B Sing the song.

C Can singing this song make you feel like a community leader?

Drawing a Cityscape

A cityscape is a type of painting in which the artist represents scenes of life in a city.

When painting a cityscape, it is important to use perspective. Perspective involves using lines to make some objects appear closer and others farther away. Artists do this on a flat surface by making things bigger at the bottom to make them seem closer, and smaller at the top so they appear to be in the distance.

This example of a cityscape is by Mark McMahon, a well-known painter from Chicago. His painting brings the city of Chicago to life by making it appear that the street goes off into the distance away from the viewer.

A Draw a cityscape.

1. Look through magazines and postcards to find a photograph of a city scene.

2. Start by drawing the outline of the streets and buildings, using a pencil.

3. Next, draw details, such as windows and doors on the buildings.

Supplies

- white art paper
- pencil and eraser
- crayons or colored pencils
- old travel magazines and postcards

B Describe how your cityscape is the same as and different from McMahon's cityscape. Be sure to include details about how you used perspective to create the illusion of distance.

Impressions

Local ★ ★ Government

The local government makes laws for a city or town. It has departments that provide services for the people living there. Some of those departments include police, fire, and parks. The leader of a city or town is often called the mayor. The mayor works in a building that is usually called city hall or town hall.

A Share with the class some details about the community you live in and some of the departments and services your community provides.

B Using a Venn diagram, compare your community in the United States with the community in which your parents or grandparents were raised.

1. What was the local government like?

2. What services were provided to the people?

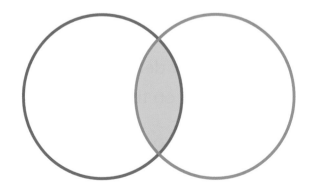

Your Editorial

▶ Write four paragraphs about an issue that is important to your community.
Include the following:

- a description of the issue
- the reason it is important
- what local government can do about it
- what the community can do about it
- your personal opinion about what to do

The Writing Process

Remember, the writing process includes a series of steps:

- **Developing Ideas** Use the Internet, visual elements, or other references to help you gather and develop ideas.

- **Organizing** Choose the ideas you want to use. Put them in order, connect them, or discard the least important ones.

- **Drafting** Use the ideas you organized to write paragraphs.

- **Revising** Read your paragraphs again and correct your writing, keeping in mind what you learned in this unit.

- **Rewriting** Produce a clean copy of your piece, applying all the corrections, to display in class.

Remember, you can always repeat a step if you need to.

Unit 5 The World Around Us

To remember the names of the planets in order, according to their distance from the Sun, memorize this sentence:
Most Vocal Exercises Make Jingles Sound Unbelievably Normal.
(Mercury, Venus, Earth, Mars, Jupiter, Saturn, Uranus, Neptune).

Topics to explore:

▶ planets and the solar system

▶ continents and landforms

▶ phases of the Moon

Spotlight on Reading

Key Words

fox
mountain
moonlight
desert
mole
creatures
soil
crescent
insects
braiding
owl
condor

Predicting

Answer the questions in complete sentences.

1. What clues do the key words provide about what might happen in the story?

2. What does the illustration tell you about where the story might take place?

3. What does the title tell you the story might be about?

Fox and Mole

Retold by Mario Castro

Illustrated by Emiliano Ordás

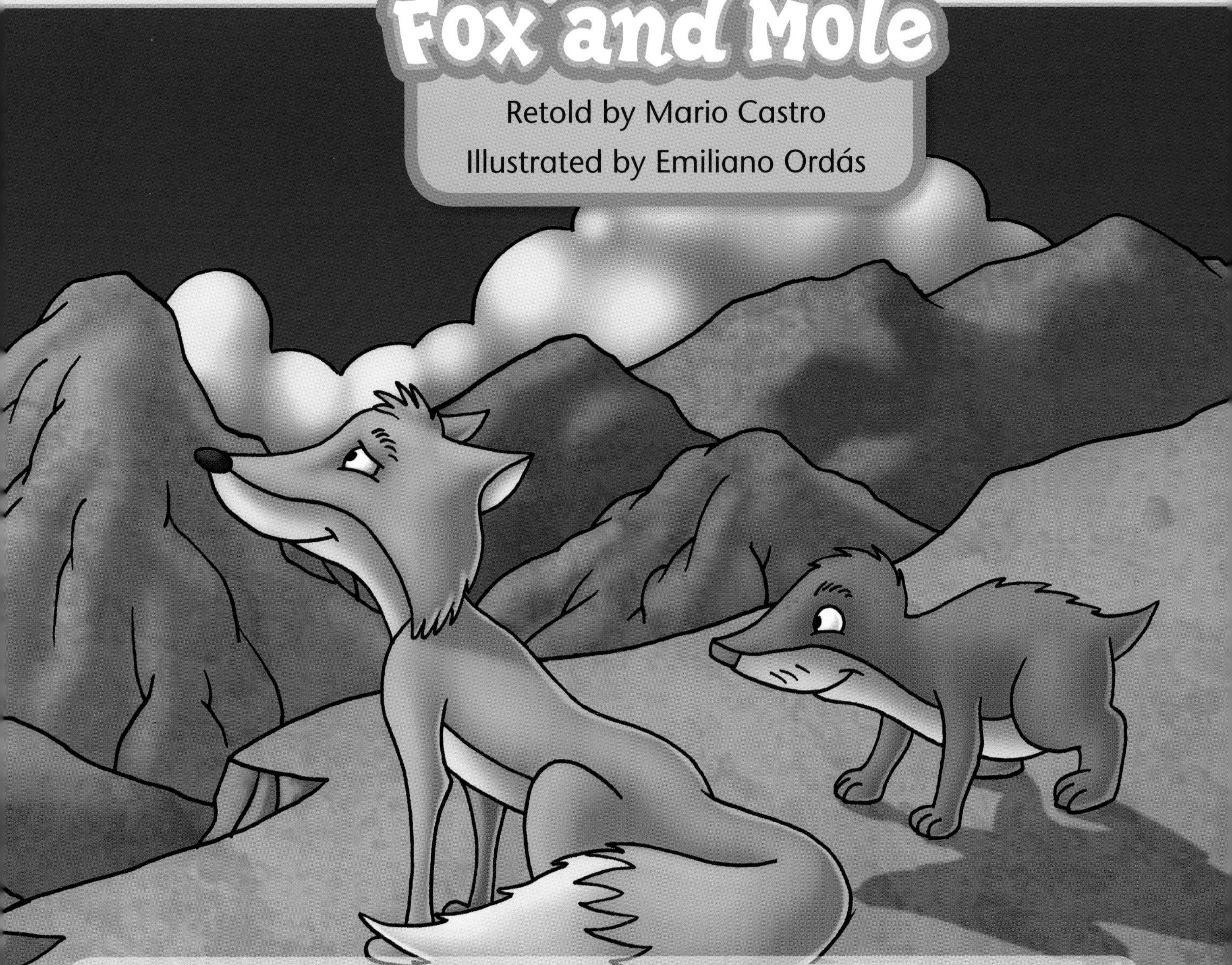

When the curtain opens, Fox is sitting on top of a mountain, looking up at the Full Moon. There is moonlight everywhere. It shines on the mountains and on the desert far away.

Narrator: Once upon a time, Fox and Mole were best friends. They watched the Moon change its shape in the sky, and they crossed plains and mountains together.

Mole [*arriving*]: I knew I would find you here. What are you doing, Fox?

Fox: Hi, Mole. Oh, nothing. I was just looking at this really beautiful Full Moon and thinking. Tell me, what is the greatest wish you have ever had?

Mole: I have always wished for one thing … to find delicious creatures in the soil! My favorites are worms, slugs, and grubs. They are so fat and juicy! Yum! What about you? What is your greatest wish?

Fox [*sighs*]: My greatest wish is to go to the Moon. It's so beautiful. Imagine all the things you can see from the Moon.

Mole: That's crazy! Where do you get these ideas? Do you think you can just fly there? Guess what, you don't have wings! So how are you going to get to the Moon?

Fox: Well, I have an idea. We'll make a very long rope, we'll wait for the Crescent Moon and throw the rope around the tip of the Moon. Then we can climb up there.

Mole: That could work! Wait a second! What do you mean "we"?

Fox: You and I, Mole.

Mole: There is no way I'm going to the Moon with you.
Why do you think I want to go to the Moon?
When did you ever hear me say I wanted to go to the Moon?
Why do I always have to help with these crazy plans
of yours, Fox? Someone is going to get hurt, and that
someone is always me!

Fox: By the way, did I tell you there are insects on the Moon?

Mole: Insects on the Moon? Now you have my full attention!
Are there lots on the Moon?

Fox: Well, let's say a lot more than you can eat.

Mole: All I can eat? That's a lot! Are you sure? [*Fox nods his head yes.*]
This could be interesting and delicious. Okay, let's try it!
But I still think it's a really crazy idea. These better be great insects!

Narrator: The next night, Fox and Mole started to work on the rope.
Using some very strong plants, they worked many days and nights
twisting and braiding them to make the rope. When it was finished,
all they had to do was wait for the Crescent Moon to come.

Fox: Look, Mole. The Moon is perfect now. This is our chance!

Mole: All right. Just twirl the rope around your head a few times and then,
throw it as hard and as high as you can.

[*Fox throws the rope as both look up, but it falls on Mole's face.*]

Mole: Thanks, Fox. Nice try, but I think we're going to need a longer rope.
Try throwing with your other paw.

Fox: I'm sorry, Mole. I didn't mean to get the rope around your nose!
Why don't we climb to the top of the highest mountain?
I'm sure we won't miss from there.

Owl [*appearing up in a tree*]: Hi, guys. What are you two up to?

Mole: Not much, Owl. We are just trying to tie this rope around the Moon.

Owl: Why in the world do you want to do that?

Fox: Because I want to go to the Moon, and my friend Mole is going with me. He's going to have a delicious dinner of Moon insects when we get there.

Owl: Oh, really? Well, you should ask a bird to carry the rope to the Moon and tie it for you.

Mole: Owl, you're a bird. Can you help us?

Owl: No, I can't help you, but Condor flies higher than any other bird. Go see him. He's perfect! If you ask him nicely, I'm sure he will be glad to help.

Fox: Of course! Why didn't I think of Condor before? Let's go, Mole.

Narrator: By the time Fox and Mole found Condor, it was almost daylight.

Condor [*looking down at Fox and Mole*]: What are you doing here? It's morning. Look at the rising Sun! Are you lost? You two are night creatures. You should be sleeping now!

Fox: Condor, we came to ask you a favor.

Mole: We know you can fly as high as the Moon, and we want you to fly there and tie this rope around the Moon.

Condor: The Moon! Are you sure you want me to do this?

Fox: Yes, Condor! Please do this for us.

Condor: All right, but if you fall, I'm not going to save you.

Narrator: That night, Condor flew up to the Moon carrying one end of the rope. He tied it to the Crescent Moon and then waved to Fox and Mole.

Fox: Okay, Mole. Let's tie this end of the rope to a tree and start climbing.

Mole: I don't know, Fox … It seems so high. I'm a little scared.

Fox: Just follow me and think about all those insects on the Moon.

Narrator: Fox starts to climb, and Mole follows slowly behind. Soon he starts to feel dizzy.

Mole: Hey, Fox. Are we almost there? I'm getting dizzy. I'm hungry, and I'm really afraid.

Fox: Then don't look down. We need to climb a little higher.

Mole: How much higher? This is getting too scary! What if I fall? No more delicious worms, no more juicy grubs, no more [*he gulps*] ... Mole!

Fox: Calm down! You worry too much. Just hang on to the rope and don't look down! We are almost there.

Mole: How do you know? How can you see anything with these thick clouds around us?

Fox: I can see just fine. Before long we will be there. Focus, Mole, focus!

Narrator: Finally, Fox and Mole got past the clouds. Then Mole looked down and got so dizzy that he let go of the rope. He was falling all the way down when fortunately Condor caught him.

Mole [*on Condor's back*]: Oh thank you, Condor.

Wait a minute! I thought you said you were not going to save us.

Condor: Mole, you're a nice guy. I know this trip to the Moon was not really your idea. You were going with Fox because he's your good friend. I changed my mind when I saw you falling. I'll take you home.

Mole: Oh no! The other animals are going to make fun of me! I don't want to see them. I can never show my face again. I'm so ashamed, Condor!

Narrator: Mole was very embarrassed. As soon as Condor dropped him on Earth, he dug a tunnel to hide in. He went deep underground and has been living there ever since, and he never shows his face to the other animals. Meanwhile, Fox is still on the Moon, living happily where he always wanted to be. When the Moon is full, you just might be able to see the happy fox in his home on the Moon.

Checking

A Choose the correct answer.

1. Mole's greatest wish is …
   a. to go to the Moon.
   b. to be best friends with Fox forever.
   c. to find delicious creatures in the soil.
   d. to fly on the back of Condor.

2. How do Fox and Mole plan to get to the Moon?
   a. They plan to make wings out of bird feathers.
   b. They plan to tie a very long rope around the Moon and then, climb up the rope.
   c. They plan to ask Owl how to do it.
   d. They plan to climb on Condor's back, and he will fly them to the Moon.

3. Who caught Mole after he fell off the rope?
   a. Fox caught Mole.   c. Condor caught Mole.
   b. Owl caught Mole.   d. Nobody caught Mole.

4. Why did Mole dig a tunnel once he returned to Earth?
   a. He wanted darkness so that he could sleep.
   b. He was looking for soil creatures.
   c. He was hiding from Condor so that he wouldn't be eaten.
   d. He was embarrassed and didn't want to show his face.

B Answer the Critical Thinking questions in complete sentences.

1. Why do you think Fox wanted Mole to go with him to the Moon?

2. Why do you think Mole believed Fox and agreed to go to the Moon with him?

Summarizing

A Fill in the Sequence graphic organizer.

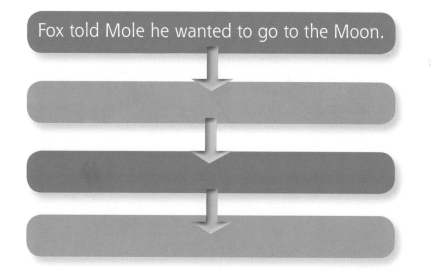

Fox told Mole he wanted to go to the Moon.

1. In the first box write about the conversation between Fox and Mole.

2. In the subsequent boxes, write what Fox and Mole did to go to the Moon.

3. In the last box write what happened to Mole.

B When you finish, use the information in your graphic organizer to write a summary of the story.

Reflecting

A Answer the questions in complete sentences.

1. Why do you think Fox wanted to go to the Moon?

2. What is the greatest wish that you have ever had?

B Write sentences that describe how you feel about the Moon or what you think of it. Read your sentences to the class.

Spotlight on Language

Connecting

A Listen to the animals.

Key Words

cities
knives
leaves
skies
stories
talons
tunnels
wolves

B Answer the questions in complete sentences.

1. What wild animals are closely related to dogs?

2. In what kinds of communities do you find many tall buildings?

Focusing

A Write the missing captions below the pictures.

one leaf   _____   one daisy   _____

B Rewrite the following sentences correctly by changing the underlined word to its correct form.

1. Children should not play with kitchen <u>knife</u>.

2. There are many books with great <u>story</u> in the library.

3. My grandmother has lived in many different <u>city</u>.

Applying

▶ Write two paragraphs about stories you have read in class and on your own.

1. In the first paragraph describe stories you have liked and explain why you have liked them.

2. In the second paragraph describe stories you have not liked and explain why you haven't liked them.

3. Read your paragraphs to the class.

I have liked many of the stories read in class because ...

I have not liked the scary stories because ...

Connecting

 A Read and listen to the conversation between Owl and Condor.

 Owl: Remember the day you flew to the Moon with the rope Fox and Mole made?

Condor: That was the easy part.

Owl: Easy for you because you have such big wings and can fly so high.

Condor: Think how long it took Fox and Mole to make that rope.

Owl: A very long time, I'm sure.

Condor: And poor Mole. Fox made him believe that the Moon was full of insects.

Owl: I almost said to Mole that what Fox was telling him was not true. I knew Fox was lying.

Condor: I felt sorry for Mole when I saw him falling down.

Owl: You were very kind to Mole. You saved him and brought him back to Earth alive.

Condor: I don't know what Mole was thinking. Wherever Fox went, Mole followed. I wonder if he misses Fox.

Owl: All I know is that Mole is somewhere around eating insects. But I wonder what kind of food Fox is having on the Moon. I'm sure he ate better when he lived on Earth.

Condor: Well, it has been a year since Fox left. I hope he found food on the Moon!

 B Answer the questions in complete sentences.

1. Where did you go last weekend?

2. What did you see there?

3. What did you eat for dinner last night?

Focusing

▶ Choose the correct word to complete each sentence.

1. a. Mole _____ insects all the time. (eats/ate)

   b. Today Mole is sick because last night he _____ too many insects. (eats/ate)

2. a. Do you want to _____ to the Moon? (went/go)

   b. Fox _____ to the Moon a year ago. (went/go)

3. a. Most birds _____, but not all. (fly/flew)

   b. José _____ on an airplane to visit his grandparents. (fly/flew)

4. a. I _____ full after eating dinner. (feels/felt)

   b. The sandpaper _____ rough. (feels/felt)

5. a. Owls can _____ well at night. (see/saw)

   b. Mole _____ Fox looking up at the Moon. (see/saw)

Applying

▶ Write a paragraph.

1. Talk to a partner about something you wished for when you were younger.

2. Take notes about your partner's wish, and then write about it.

3. Review the paragraph. Ask yourself: *Will a reader understand that I wrote about something my partner wished for in the past?*

My partner always wanted to go to the Moon.

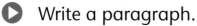

Connecting

(A) Read the passage.

Every now and then I think about Mole. When I lived on Earth, he followed me everywhere. I hope he is all right. The other day when the Moon was full, I tried to look for him. I stretched and stretched in the direction of Earth, and I opened my eyes as wide as possible. I looked for Mole for a long time. I wanted to see him. I wanted to make sure he was all right. But he is so small, and I am so far away.

I dreamed that Condor visited me. We talked about Mole. I asked him what happened. Condor explained to me how Mole was falling down and Condor saved him. I asked Condor to come back with Mole, but then some noise awakened me, and I stopped dreaming.

(B) Answer the questions in complete sentences.

1. What did your teacher explain to you about this lesson?

2. What did you dream about last night?

3. What did you want for breakfast this morning?

Focusing

▶ Choose the correct word from each pair to complete the sentences.

1. a. Fox _____ about Condor last night. (dreams/dreamed)

    b. John _____ of becoming an astronaut. (dreams/dreamed)

2. a. My mother always _____ at red lights. (stops/stopped)

    b. Mole got dizzy and _____ climbing the rope. (stops/stopped)

3. a. Condor _____ Mole and carried him back home. (save/saved)

    b. Lifeguards _____ swimmers from drowning. (save/saved)

4. a. Fox _____ Mole into going to the Moon. (talk/talked)

    b. My parents _____ to my teacher every week. (talk/talked)

5. a. I _____ in the United States. (live/lived)

    b. My family _____ in Perú before coming to the United States.
        (live/lived)

Applying

▶ Write a paragraph that describes, in your own words, things
that Mole and Fox did together. Start your paragraph with a
general idea. Then, add specific details.

Fox and Mole talked about
the Moon.

Expository Writing

The Moon

The light that we see on the Moon comes from the Sun. Sunlight bounces off the surface of the Moon and becomes moonlight. The Moon appears to have different phases, or shapes. But actually the Moon is always round, like a sphere. What happens is that, from Earth, we see only the parts of the Moon that are facing the Sun as the Moon circles Earth. It takes the Moon 29.5 days to go around Earth. As the Moon does this, it goes through its phases.

The phases of the Moon include New Moon, Crescent Moon, and Full Moon. When we can't see the Moon at all, we call it a New Moon.

A Crescent Moon is when we see only an edge of the lighted side of the Moon, and a Full Moon is when we see the entire half of the Moon that is lighted by the Sun.

New Moon

Crescent Moon

Full Moon

▶ Answer the questions in complete sentences.

1. What is the main idea of this passage?

2. Does this passage give facts or opinions?

3. How do the illustrations support the written text?

Writing an Expository Text

Expository writing gives information about a topic. It defines, describes, and explains it. Often the writer needs to research his or her topic to obtain information. This kind of writing must be simple, clear, and well organized. Pictures can be used to support the text and help the reader understand it.

Tips for writing an expository text:

- Research your topic to obtain interesting information for the reader.
- Organize the information around two or three main ideas about the topic.
- Be sure each paragraph refers to one main idea.
- Be sure to include factual evidence to support each main idea.
- Consider using pictures to support the written text.

▶ Write four paragraphs about an object in the sky that interests you, such as a planet, a comet, or a star.

1. In the first paragraph, introduce the object in a way that will interest the reader.

2. In the second and third paragraphs, provide information about the object.

3. Use illustrations to support your writing and make it easier to understand.

4. For your fourth paragraph, write a conclusion.

Key Words

expository
research
support
topic

Capitalization and Punctuation

Capitalization Rules:

- Capitalize the first letter of the first word in a sentence.

  The story is about a fox and a mole.

- Capitalize proper nouns, or the names of people, places, and important things.

  Neil Armstrong walked on the Moon.

- Words used as names are also capitalized.

  Fox   Mole   Owl   Condor   Dad

- The pronoun "I" is always capitalized.

  Yesterday my friend and I went to the library.

- Months, days of the week, and holidays are capitalized.

  Thanksgiving is always the third Thursday in November.

Punctuation Rules:

- Use a period at the end of a declarative sentence.

  We are learning how to use capital letters.

- Use a comma between items in a series (or list) of three items or more.

  The Sun, the Moon, and Earth are in space.

- Use a comma before a word that connects two sentences (and, or, nor, but, for, so, yet)

  Mario wants to go to the movies, but Mónica disagrees.

- Use a comma to separate an introductory word or a phrase at the beginning of a sentence.

  When I was on vacation, I went to the beach every day.

▼ Key Words

comma
declarative
period
proper nouns

▶ Rewrite the following sentences with the correct capitalization and punctuation.

1. there is no life on the moon so nothing grows on it

2. i live near the mountains in albuquerque new mexico

3. there is no school on saturday or sunday

4. michael collins and buzz aldrin went to the moon with neil armstrong

5. my friends juanita karla and lupe want to be astronauts

6. my favorite stories this year have been the world's greatest sandwich and fox and mole

7. after i finish third grade i will be in fourth grade

Revising

A Review the expository text you wrote to complete the activity on page 165.

- What research did you do to write about an object in space?

- What did you do to write down your findings in an interesting and clear way?

- What is the main idea in each paragraph?

- What words did you capitalize?

- Did you use periods and commas correctly?

- Did you consider including a picture?

B Rewrite your expository text, making any necessary corrections.

Polygons

A polygon is a type of figure with the following characteristics:

- The figure is on a plane, or flat, surface.
- It has two dimensions, such as length and width.
- It has three or more sides, or line segments.
- It is a closed figure.
- It can have a different number of sides and angles.

To find out how long a polygon is all around, or its perimeter, add the lengths of its sides.

6 cm

4 cm

6 cm + 4 cm + 6 cm + 4 cm = 20 cm

To find out the space that a polygon takes up, you find its area, or the number of square units it occupies.

- To find the area of a rectangle, you multiply the number of units it measures on one side by the number of units it measures on the other. The result is expressed in square units.

6 cm

4 cm

6 cm x 4 cm = 24 square cm

Key Words

area
perimeter
polygon

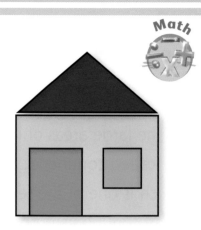

A Complete the sentences with the name of the correct polygon.

1. The roof of this house is shaped like a _____.

2. The house itself is shaped like a _____.

3. The windows are shaped like _____.

B Match the statements with the correct figures.

1. Its angles are square and all its sides are equal.

2. It is not a polygon.

3. It has two longer sides and two shorter sides.

4. It has three sides and three angles.

a.   b.   c.   d.

C Answer the questions in complete sentences.

1. A postage stamp is 4 centimeters wide by 2 centimeters high. How would you find the area of the postage stamp?

2. A basketball court is 25 meters long by 15 meters wide. How would you find the perimeter of the court?

3. If you wanted to build a fence around a field that is 18 meters long by 9 meters wide, would you need to find the area or the perimeter of that field?

Geography

The large areas of land shown on the world map are called continents. We live in North America, which is one of the seven continents. The surface of these continents is not smooth. It has many different landforms, or shapes.

The large bodies of water that surround these continents are called oceans. There are five oceans surrounding the continents. Lakes and rivers are smaller bodies of water that can be found within a continent.

Key Words

bay
bodies of water
continents
island
lake
landforms
oceans
peninsula
plain
river
valley

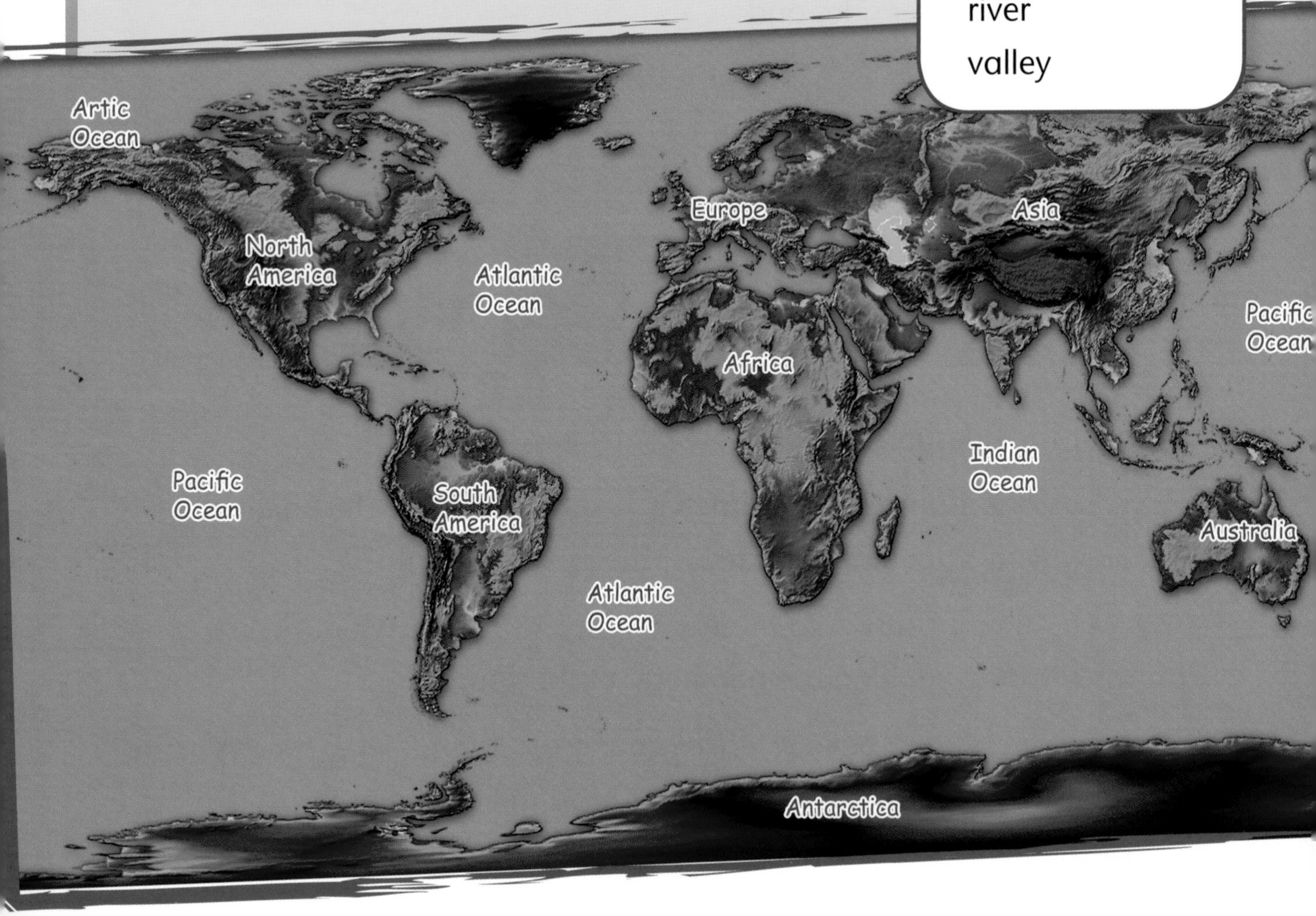

Artic Ocean

North America

Atlantic Ocean

Europe

Asia

Pacific Ocean

Africa

Indian Ocean

Pacific Ocean

South America

Australia

Atlantic Ocean

Antarctica

Bodies of Water	Landforms
• A lake is a body of water surrounded by land on all sides. • A bay is a body of water mostly, but not completely, surrounded by land. • A river is a long stream of water that flows into another body of water.	• A plain is a large area of land that is flat. • A valley is an area of land surrounded by mountains. • An island is an area of land surrounded by water on all sides. • A peninsula is an area of land surrounded by water on three sides.

Social Studies

A Use a globe or an atlas to answer the questions in complete sentences.

1. The state of Florida is a landform surrounded by water on three of its sides. What is the name of this kind of landform?

2. One of the seven continents is also an island and a country. What is the name of this continent?

3. What is the name of the body of water located between the continents of Asia, Africa, and Australia?

B Write a paragraph about a landform or a body of water.

1. Research the landform or body of water in the library or on the Internet.

2. The landform or body of water you choose can be in the United States or in a different country.

3. Include details about the landform or body of water you choose.

Objects in the Sky

There are objects in the sky that can be seen from Earth. Some of these objects are the Sun, the Moon, some planets, and stars. Stars are large balls of extremely hot gas that produce their own light. The star that is closest to Earth is the Sun.

The Sun is the center of our solar system. It provides Earth with solar energy in the form of heat and light. Without the Sun, there could not be life on Earth. Plants use the light from the Sun to make their own food. People have also recently learned to convert the power of the Sun's light and heat into electricity.

The Moon is a satellite that travels in circles around, or orbits, Earth. It is held to this path by a force called gravity. The gravity of the Moon and the Sun exert a pulling force on the water from the oceans and other large bodies of water on Earth. This pull causes tides, which are rises and falls in the level of the water every day.

Earth is a planet. In addition to Earth, there are seven other planets in our solar system. All of them circle, or orbit, the Sun. It takes Earth approximately 365 days to go around the Sun. This is why there are 365 days in one year.

A Choose the correct word to complete the sentences.

orbits   satellite   planet   star   gravity

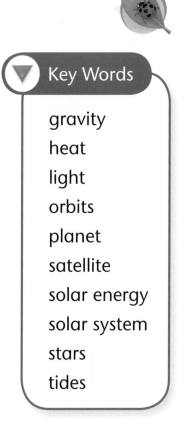

Key Words

gravity
heat
light
orbits
planet
satellite
solar energy
solar system
stars
tides

1. The Sun is a _____.

2. The Moon is a _____.

3. Earth is a _____.

4. Tides are caused by the _____ of the Moon and the Sun.

5. The Moon travels around, or _____, Earth.

B Write a paragraph that tells how objects in the sky affect life on Earth. Be sure to identify each of the objects in the sky that has an effect on Earth, and what kind of effect it has.

Sing Along

A Listen to the song.

Twinkle, Twinkle, Little Star

Twinkle, twinkle, little star,
How I wonder what you are!
Up above the world so high,
Like a diamond in the sky.
Twinkle, twinkle, little star,
How I wonder what you are!

When the blazing Sun is gone,
When it nothing shines upon,
Then you show your little light,
Twinkle, twinkle, all the night.
Twinkle, twinkle, little star,
How I wonder what you are!

B Sing the song.

C What items can you think of that twinkle, blaze, or shine?

Comparing Landscapes

Landscapes, or paintings of nature, are representations of landforms and environments. They show a background that includes sky, water, mountains, or grass. They also show natural objects in the foreground. They use color, light, and shading to differentiate what is in the background and what is in the foreground.

Vincent van Gogh

These landscapes are by Vincent van Gogh and Jean Françoise Xavier Roffiaen.

Françoise Roffiaen

A Answer the questions in complete sentences.

1. How is the foreground alike and different in each landscape?

2. How is the background alike and different in each landscape?

3. How does Van Gogh differentiate between foreground and background?

4. What is special about the way Roffiaen uses light and shadow?

Supplies

- white art paper
- pencil and eraser
- crayons or colored pencils

B Draw a landscape of some place you imagine. Then, describe how your landscape is the same as or different from those of Van Gogh and Roffiaen.

Impressions

The Colorado River

The Colorado River starts in the Rocky Mountains and flows through the Southwest. Like most rivers, it has many uses. When the river reaches the Hoover Dam, the water is used to produce electricity. Some of the water is also contained in Lake Mead. Lake Meade is an important reservoir, or water deposit, created by the dam. Water from the lake is used to irrigate large desert areas.

A Answer the questions in complete sentences.

1. Locate the Colorado River on a map of the United States. Through which states does this river flow? Do you live in one of these states? Which one?

2. Does the water you drink originally come from a river? How can you find out?

B Share the information about landforms and bodies of water from your family's country of origin. Then, answer the following questions.

1. What do you know about how people in other cultures use rivers for their benefit?

2. How are these uses similar to or different from how the Colorado River is used?

Your Expository Writing

▶ Write four paragraphs about planet Earth.
Do research to learn more about our planet before you
begin to write. Include the following in your writing:

- the location of Earth in space
- the shape of Earth and its movements
- the landforms and bodies of water found on Earth
- Earth's Moon

The Writing Process

Remember, the writing process includes a series of steps:

- **Developing Ideas** Use the Internet, visual elements, or other
  references to help you gather and develop ideas.

- **Organizing** Choose the ideas you want to use. Put them in
  order, connect them, or discard the least important ones.

- **Drafting** Use the ideas you organized to write paragraphs.

- **Revising** Read your paragraphs again and correct your
  writing, keeping in mind what you learned in this unit.

- **Rewriting** Produce a clean copy of your piece, applying
  all the corrections, to display in class.

Remember, you can always repeat a step if you need to.

Unit 6 The Natural World

Girl giraffes giggle at gestures by guy giraffes who get indigestion from enjoying goose gibblets in gravy.

Topics to explore:

▸ folktales from other countries

▸ farming and crops

▸ animals and the environment

Spotlight on Reading

Key Words

- bull
- plow
- fields
- monsoon
- season
- earthworm
- soil
- tunnels
- digest
- bucket
- pond
- bait

Predicting

Answer the questions in complete sentences.

1. What does the title tell you the story might be about?

2. What can you tell from the picture about what might happen in the story?

3. What clues do the key words give you to what the story might be about?

The Bull and the Earthworms

Retold by Betsy Tecco
Illustrated by Esteban Alfaro

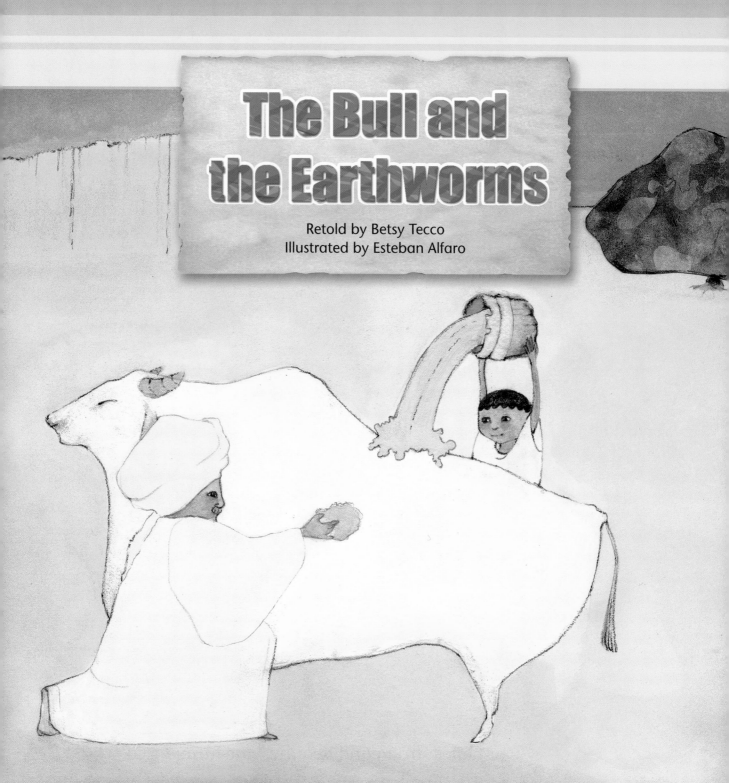

It was a hot, dry day in West Bengal, India.
A farmer and his son were giving their bull a bath.
The bull was a Zebu (zee-bu), which is a type of ox.
The farmer and his son washed the large bull's strong
legs, long ears, and big hump on his back.

"Our bull is strong and healthy," the farmer told his son. "He can plow our fields."

The ground was too hard and dry that day. The farmer and his son had to wait for monsoon season, when the big rains came. In the dry season, the bull ate grass or special food and stayed under the mango tree.

One day the bull walked across the empty wheat field. It wasn't empty; many earthworms lived deep in the soil.

"Your life is so easy, Bull," a tiny voice called up to the tall animal.

Who was that? The bull leaned closer to the ground. It was the earthworms squirming in the ground. The worms had tiny hairs called bristles on their brown bodies. They used the bristles to push in and out of the soil.

"What is so hard about your life, earthworms?
All you do is hide in the soil."

"Nobody sees how busy we are," one worm
answered. "We work hard down here while you get
treated well."

The bull snorted. "If you don't want to work,
then don't."

The bull swished his tail. He stepped over the earthworms. He walked away.

"Why should we work? The bull gets all the care and attention. Let's go!"

The worms left the wheat field. They stopped working. Some of them rested under the mango trees and didn't move.

In June the monsoon season started. Heavy rains poured down onto the dry, cracked earth. It was time to prepare the field. The farmer and his son tied the bull to a small wooden plow. The farmer noticed something wrong with the soil. His hands dug into the dirt.

"There aren't any earthworms in the soil," the farmer said.

"Is that important?" his son asked.

"They help our plants grow," the farmer explained. "They make tunnels in the ground to let air and water into the soil. Everything they eat and digest helps the soil for our crops."

"What about our wheat?" asked the son.

The farmer sighed. "It won't grow fast. It won't be big and strong without the earthworms. We must find other food."

The farmer led the bull back to the mango trees. He found the earthworms resting there. "How lazy," he thought, angrily.

"You're in trouble now," the bull said to the earthworms. "Your work was important to the farmer. You're not working, and he is very angry."

The farmer returned with his son. They pulled the earthworms from the ground and put them in a bucket. They took the bucket and two fishing poles to the pond.

"We can't eat wheat," said the farmer. "But we can eat fish. And we can use the worms as bait!"

The earthworms squirmed. They wanted to hide, but they were trapped in the bucket.

"It was a mistake! We miss working in the field," the worms told the farmer. "It is much better to feed the soil than feed a hungry fish! Please, give us another chance!"

Checking

A Choose the correct answer.

1. Why are the father and son bathing the bull when the story begins?
    a. Because the bull has been sick.
    b. Because the weather is hot.
    c. Because the farmer hates the bull.
    d. Because the bull is full of dirt.

2. What does the bull tell the earthworms?
    a. Don't help the farmer.
    b. Get the soil ready to plant wheat.
    c. Look out or I will step on you.
    d. Don't work if you don't want to.

3. Why is the farmer angry at the earthworms?
    a. He thinks the earthworms are being lazy.
    b. He thinks the earthworms eat too much fruit.
    c. He thinks the earthworms upset the bull.
    d. He thinks the earthworms don't like his son.

4. Why do the farmer and his son put the earthworms in a bucket?
    a. The bull tells them to do it.
    b. They want to use the earthworms as fish bait.
    c. The soil is too hard for worms to live in.
    d. The son wants to save the worms.

B Answer the Critical Thinking questions in complete sentences.

1. How can you tell the bull and the earthworms do not like each other?

2. Should the farmer give the earthworms another chance?
    Why or why not?

Summarizing

A Fill in the Cause and Effect graphic organizer.

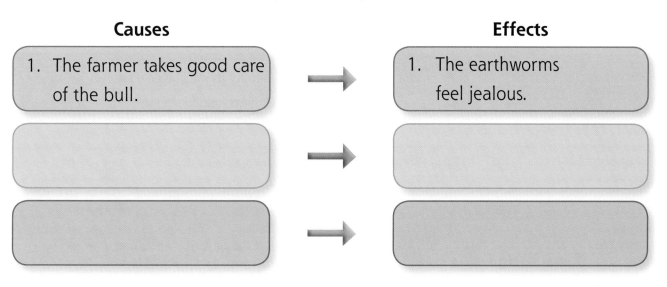

Causes

1. The farmer takes good care of the bull.

Effects

1. The earthworms feel jealous.

1. In the boxes on the left, describe the event that causes something else to happen.

2. In the boxes on the right, describe the event that is the effect or result of the event you described in the box on the left.

B Use the information in your graphic organizer to write a summary of the story.

Reflecting

A Answer the questions in complete sentences.

1. Was the father's idea to use the earthworms for fishing good or bad? Explain your answer.

2. What lesson can you learn from this story?

3. How can you apply this lesson to your own life?

B Write three reasons why it is important to do your schoolwork. Read your reasons to the class.

Connecting

A Listen to the conversation between the farmer and the earthworms.

What things will you do if I don't feed you to the fish?

Key Words

will be
will do
will feel
will give
will listen
will make
will stay
will take
will work

B Answer the questions in complete sentences.

1. What will you do after school this afternoon?

2. Where will you go this weekend?

Focusing

▶ Rewrite the sentences so that the action will happen later or at a future time, according to the conversation.

1. The boy gives the earthworms another chance.

2. The earthworms make tunnels in the soil.

3. The bull stays under the mango tree.

4. The farmer and the boy work hard.

5. The bull listens to the farmer.

6. The soil feels soft with the rain.

Applying

Ⓐ Write a paragraph about things you will do in the next few days. To get started, ask yourself questions such as *What day will it be tomorrow? What will I do tomorrow? What day will it be the day after tomorrow? What will I do the day after tomorrow?*

Ⓑ Read your paragraph to the class.

Tomorrow I will ...
The day after tomorrow I will ...
The weekend will be ...

Connecting

 A Read and listen to the boy's conversation with the animals.

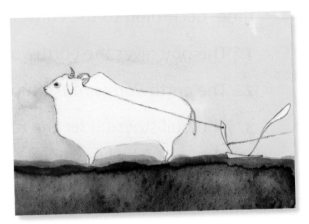

There are many things we can do on this farm. Look, my father can bathe Bull.

You, Bull, are the strongest one on this farm. You can help turn over the soil. You can pull the plow.

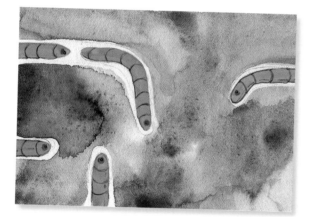

And you, worms, tell me what you can do. "We can move around in the soil and make tunnels. Then, when it rains, the soil can absorb water better."

I can go fishing with my father, but I don't like to fish.

B Answer the questions in complete sentences.

1. What is something you can do very well?

2. What is something you can't do very well?

Focusing

▶ Write sentences about what each character can do.

1. Bull …

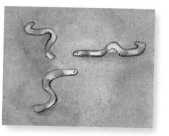

3. The earthworms …

2. The father …

4. The son …

Applying

A Make an *I can do it!* poster.

1. Draw and color three or four things you can do at school or at home.

2. Write a sentence to describe each picture.

3. Sign your poster.

B Share your poster with the class.

Connecting

A Read about growing wheat.

wheat

Wheat is one of the crops that farmers started to grow thousands and thousands of years ago. These farmers didn't have tools made of metal, and they didn't have tractors.

Today we're still growing wheat. But the way we do it has changed. Let's look at the way we grow wheat now. I'm a modern farmer with a tractor. I don't need a bull to plow the fields. But growing wheat is never easy.

A farmer can't grow wheat when the soil is hard and dry. A farmer doesn't know what the weather is going to be like while the wheat grows. If it's too hot or too cold, or too wet or too dry, the wheat won't grow strong.

I know I have to grow wheat year after year. I'll do it because without wheat we can't have bread, cookies, flour tortillas, and many other foods.

B Answer the questions in complete sentences.

1. What are you and your family doing this weekend?

2. Is today Wednesday? If not, what day is it?

3. What sports do you like and what sports don't you like?

Focusing

A Choose the correct word or words to complete each sentence.

> it's   won't   I'll   doesn't   We're

1. _____ do my homework after supper.

2. _____ in school right now.

3. It _____ snow today because _____ too warm.

4. The farmer with a tractor _____ need a bull.

B Change the underlined words in each sentence to a single word with an apostrophe (').

1. Farmers <u>do not</u> know how the weather will be during the wheat's growing season.

2. Wheat <u>cannot</u> grow without soil, sunlight, and water.

3. <u>We are</u> learning about how farmers grow wheat.

4. <u>I am</u> going to be a farmer when I grow up.

Applying

▶ Write sentences about things that farmers could and could not do many years ago, and things that farmers can do today. Remember to use words with an apostrophe (') in the sentences you write.

Farmers can't plant wheat in hard soil.

Friendly Letter

> 1155 Quincy Avenue
> Fresno, CA 93720
> May 10, 2008
>
> Dear Bob,
>
> How are you? I am fine. Life here on the farm is good. I helped my father turn over the soil early in the spring. He added a lot of compost to make the soil rich. Soon we will have fresh vegetables to sell at our vegetable stand.
>
> Do you want to come visit me? We can have lots of fun. We live near a national park called Yosemite. It's a great place. We can go hiking, camping, and rock climbing. There are also many animals in the park. We usually stay at a cabin, so you would not need a sleeping bag or tent.
>
> Well, I hope you're doing well. Please write back when you have time.
>
> Your friend,
> Luis

Luis Armas
684 SE 28th Avenue
Columbus, OH 43268

Bob Mal
1155 Q
Fresn

▶ Answer the questions in complete sentences.

1. Whom is the letter written to?

2. When was the letter written?

3. What is the purpose of the letter?

4. Who wrote the letter?

▼ Key Words

body
closing
heading
salutation
signature

Writing a Friendly Letter

A friendly letter is one way of staying in touch with friends and family members, and also a way to make new friends.

A friendly letter follows a format that consists of five parts:

- **Heading** It is the place for your address and the date you write the letter.

- **Salutation** It is a greeting that usually starts with the word *Dear* followed by the name of the person you are writing to, and a comma.

- **Body** It is the main part of the letter, where you write what you want to say to the person you are writing to.

- **Closing** It is the way you say *good-bye*, usually with the words *Sincerely*, *Love*, or *Your friend*, followed by a comma.

- **Signature** It is the place for your name at the end of the letter.

▶ Write a friendly letter to a friend or family member.

1. Write the heading and salutation.

2. Write the body. Ask yourself what you want to tell the person you are writing to. Then, write it in a clear and organized way.

3. Write an ending to the body of your letter.

4. Write the closing and sign your letter.

218 NW 623 Drive
Hollywood, FL 33184
April 18th, 2008

Dear Jill,

You can't believe the things I can sleep on the sofa. Or we can break! I went campir and pretend we are in the wilderness. Please and wheat cr in my bed, and I can tell my parents. a hor sleeping outside and go to those places I told sleep outside and come so I can tell my parents. let me know when you can come. They can ask for vacation. Don't forget to write to me soon.

Sincerely,
Andrea

Affixes

An affix is a word part that can change the meaning of a word. Some affixes are attached to the beginning of a word, and others are attached to the end. Knowing the meaning of an affix helps you understand words that may look unfamiliar at first.

An affix attached to the beginning of a word is called a prefix. An affix attached to the end of a word is called a suffix.

Prefix	Meaning	Example
re-	to do something again	My mother **re**painted the stand.
un-	not	The farmer was **un**happy.
tri-	three	A **tri**angle has three sides.

An affix attached to the end of a word is called a suffix.

Suffix	Meaning	Example
-ful	full of	The vegetable stand is color**ful**.
-ly	manner or way	Eggs break easi**ly**.
-s	more than one	He bought twelve egg**s**.

A Circle the words that have an affix in the following sentences. Then, classify them by prefix or suffix.

1. My family has a beautiful fishing boat.

2. We can't get on the boat if we're not wearing life jackets.

3. Hard rain is unusual at this time of the year.

4. The farmer replanted some crops.

5. The Mexican flag is tricolor; it's red, white, and green.

6. We were late for class, so we walked quickly.

B Replace each underlined phrase with a single word that has an affix.

1. My teacher didn't like my essay. I have to <u>write it again</u>.

2. I'm <u>not able</u> to ride my bicycle because the tires are flat.

3. Where I live, the sunsets are <u>full of color</u>.

Revising

A Review the letter you wrote to complete the activity on page 199.

- Did you follow the letter format and include all five parts?

- Did you use words with affixes to simplify your writing? Which words have prefixes? Which words have affixes?

- Did you put a comma at the end of the salutation and the closing?

B Rewrite your friendly letter, making any necessary corrections.

Multiplication and Division

- Multiplication is the operation of adding a number to itself a specific number of times. The numbers being multiplied are called factors. The first factor is the number being added to itself, and the second factor tells how many times the number is being added to itself. The product is the number that results from multiplying the factors.

  Example: 2   x   3   =   6

             two   times   three   equals   six

  2 and 3 are the factors; 6 is the product.

- Division is the operation of separating, or dividing, a number into equal parts. The dividend is the number being divided. The divisor is the number that will divide the dividend into equal parts. The quotient is the number that results from dividing the dividend by the divisor. If the divisor does not go into the dividend evenly, the quotient will have a remainder.

  Example: 6   ÷   3   =   2

            six   divided by three   equals   two

  6 is the dividend, 3 is the divisor, and 2 is the quotient.

- A fact family of multiplication and division includes four facts, two multiplication and two division, using the same three numbers.

  Example: 2   x   3   =   6

               3   x   2   =   6

               6   ÷   3   =   2

               6   ÷   2   =   3

Key Words

divided by
dividend
division
divisor
factors
multiplication
product
quotient
remainder
times

Math

A Complete the following activities.

1. Read the number sentences aloud.

   a. $3 \times 4 =$ 12

   b. $10 \div 2 =$ 5

   c. $2 \times 3 =$ 6

   d. $9 \div 3 =$ 3

2. Complete the fact families with multiplication and division sentences.

$3 \times 5 =$	15
$5 \times 3 =$	15
$15 \div 5 =$	3

$4 \times 2 =$	8
$8 \div 4 =$	2

B Answer the questions in complete sentences.

1. Greenville Farm harvested 2 bushels of wheat per week for 3 weeks. Crescent Farm harvested 3 bushels of wheat per week for 2 weeks. How would you figure out how many bushels of wheat each farm harvested?

2. Jen planted 3 apple trees per hour for 5 hours. She did this for 3 days. How could you figure out how many trees Jen planted?

3. Jen has an avocado tree. She picks twelve avocados. She and two friends want avocados for dinner. How could you figure out how many avocados you could give to each person, so they all have the same number of avocados?

Animals in Danger

Natural resources are any things found in nature that can be used for human benefit. Natural resources include food, fibers, clean water, clean air, wildlife habitats, fertile soils, and scenic landscapes.

When people use too much of a natural resource or use a natural resource in a negative way, it can harm the environment. This can affect the animals that live in these areas. All over the world, animals are endangered. This means that they are in danger of becoming extinct. They will disappear from Earth if people don't start to use natural resources more responsibly.

One important reason animals become endangered is loss of habitat. Animals lose their homes because land developers cut down trees in forests or drain water from wetlands to make room for human needs. Animals in the wild no longer have their natural shelter from elements and predators, and they lose their sources of food.

Pollution of lakes and rivers is another reason animals become endangered. One way the water becomes polluted and harmful to animals is by the use of pesticides. People use pesticides to get rid of insects on farms. Some of the pesticide runs off into lakes and rivers when it rains. Then, the pesticide poisons animals that live in the water or drink it.

People can help conserve natural resources and learn to care for them. When people conserve, they use natural resources in a responsible way. They don't waste them. If people do not use natural resources responsibly, they can become endangered, too.

A Answer the questions in complete sentences.

1. Why are water and air natural resources?

2. What can happen when people overuse natural resources?

3. What is one way people make animal habitats disappear?

4. What is one way people make water harmful?

B Match each word with its meaning.

1. pesticide   a. substance harmful to the environment

2. habitat   b. at risk of disappearing

3. conservation   c. way of using natural resources in a responsible way

4. endangered   d. natural place in which animals live

C Use a Venn diagram to compare and contrast how people and animals use natural resources.

1. Label the left-side area *Animals*, the shared area *Both*, and the right-side area *People*.

2. List resources that are useful to both animals and people in the *Both* area.

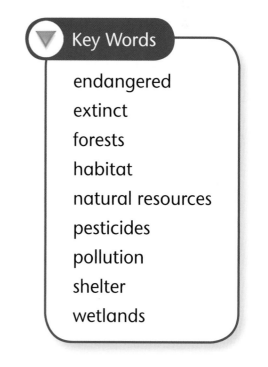

Key Words

endangered
extinct
forests
habitat
natural resources
pesticides
pollution
shelter
wetlands

Organisms

An organism is any living thing. Plants, animals, and human beings are organisms. Organisms go through a sequence of growth and change called a life cycle. They also have the ability to reproduce or make other organisms like themselves. Everything that surrounds an organism is its environment. Weather conditions and food sources are part of an organism's environment.

Organisms are divided, or classified, according to traits, or characteristics, they have in common. Animals are classified into two main groups: vertebrates and invertebrates. Vertebrates have a backbone and invertebrates do not. Animals such as cows and dogs are vertebrates; animals such as earthworms and butterflies are invertebrates.

Vertebrates are also divided into groups according to such traits as what they look like, what they eat, and where they live.

Fish are one kind of vertebrate. They live in water and are born from eggs. Typically, fish have fins they use for swimming. They use gills to get oxygen from the water. Fish are also cold-blooded, meaning that their body temperature matches the temperature of their environment.

Mammals are another type of vertebrate. Most mammals have fur or hair on their bodies and are born live, rather than from eggs. Mammals feed milk to their young, and they are warm-blooded. Their bodies stay the same temperature no matter in which environment they live. Human beings are mammals.

Birds are also vertebrates. Like fish, they are born from eggs. Birds are covered with feathers and have wings, which most of them use for flying. They also have differently shaped beaks, depending on the kind of food they eat. Like mammals, birds are warm-blooded animals.

A Choose the correct word to complete the sentences.

environment   organism   backbone

1. Every living thing is an _____ .

2. Organisms live in an _____ .

3. Invertebrates do not have a _____ .

B Answer the riddles with the name of the correct animal.

bird   cow   fish   earthworm

1. I am a mammal. I have four legs and fur. People drink my milk. What am I?

2. I am a vertebrate. I have a beak, feathers, and wings. What am I?

3. I am an invertebrate. I live in the ground. I usually make tunnels as I move through the soil. What am I?

4. I am a vertebrate. I live in the water. I have gills. What am I?

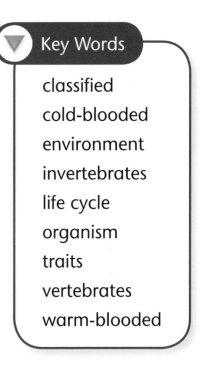

Key Words

classified
cold-blooded
environment
invertebrates
life cycle
organism
traits
vertebrates
warm-blooded

C Copy and complete the chart about three different kinds of vertebrates. Find the information in the reading.

type of vertebrate	way it gets around	body covering	environment
mammals			
fish			
birds			

Sing Along

A Listen to the song.

Down by the Bay

Down by the bay,
Where the watermelons grow,
Back to my home, I dare not go.
For if I do, my mother will say,
"Did you ever see a bear
Combing his hair
Down by the bay?"

Down by the bay,
Where the watermelons grow,
Back to my home, I dare not go.
For if I do, my mother will say,
"Did you ever see a bee
With a cup of tea
Down by the bay?"

Down by the bay,
Where the watermelons grow,
Back to my home, I dare not go.
For if I do, my mother will say,
"Did you ever see an ox
Wearing red socks
Down by the bay?"

Down by the bay,
Where the watermelons grow,
Back to my home, I dare not go.
For if I do, my mother will say,
"Did you ever see a fish
Jump off a dish
Down by the bay?"

B Sing the song.

C Answer the questions in complete sentences.

1. What animals are named in the song?

2. What words in the song are included because they rhyme
   with the names of the animals?

The Birds of Audubon

Before the camera was invented, people depended on illustrators and painters to make pictures. The painting seen here is by John James Audubon, who lived in the first half of the nineteenth century. Audubon was a naturalist and a painter. For much of his life, he devoted himself to the study of birds and made hundreds of paintings of them.

The paintings of Audubon are historic because they realistically show birds in their habitat, as he saw them during his lifetime. He traveled to various places to find unusual birds, such as the American Flamingo (shown in the painting) and the Great American Sea Eagle.

A Draw and color a picture of a bird that is familiar to you. Be sure to include realistic details, such as where the bird would live.

B Compare Audubon's painting, a modern photograph, and your drawing.

1. How are the three birds alike and different?

2. How are their environments alike and different?

3. Which bird looks more real? Why?

4. Which picture do you like best? Why?

Supplies

- white art paper
- pencil and eraser
- crayons or colored pencils

Impressions

Protecting Endangered Animals

Manatees are large, gray, herbivorous mammals found in shallow, slow-moving bodies of water. Manatees migrate, or travel from place to place, with the change in seasons. In the United States, manatees are mainly found in Florida during the winter months. Manatees graze for food along the bottom of shallow waterways and sometimes eat the plants that float on the water's surface. Submerged manatees, like whales, come to the surface of the water to breathe every three to five minutes. Because they stay so close to the surface of the water and move so slowly, manatees are sometimes hurt by passing motorboats.

Manatees in the United States are protected by the Marine Mammal Protection Act and the Endangered Species Act. They are also protected by the Florida Manatee Sanctuary Act. In addition to imposing fines for harming or killing manatees, these laws also impose speed limits to prevent motorboats from injuring the manatees.

A Answer the questions in complete sentences.

1. Why are manatees endangered?

2. What is the government doing to protect them?

B Share information about endangered animals from your family's country of origin and how they are protected.

1. What animals are safe? What animals are endangered? Why?

2. How are endangered animals being protected?

Your Friendly Letter

▶ Write a friendly letter to a pen pal about the official bird and flower of the state where you live. Include the following:

- How the bird and the flower became symbols of your state.

- A comparison between the symbols of your state and the symbols of your friend's state.

- A description of the flower, the plant it comes from, and where it grows.

- A description of the bird and its habitat.

- How the bird and the flower are cared for and protected.

The Writing Process

Remember, the writing process includes a series of steps:

- **Developing Ideas** Use the Internet, visual elements, or other references to help you gather and develop ideas.

- **Organizing** Choose the ideas you want to use. Put them in order, connect them, or discard the least important ones.

- **Drafting** Use the ideas you organized to write paragraphs.

- **Revising** Read your paragraphs again and correct your writing, keeping in mind what you learned in this unit.

- **Rewriting** Produce a clean copy of your piece, applying all the corrections, to display in class.

Remember, you can always repeat a step if you need to.

Unit 7 Heroes and Landmarks

I was the twenty-sixth president of the United States and the youngest president in the nation's history. I am now best known for my conservation efforts. When I was alive, I was a big-game hunter. On one hunting trip, I refused to shoot an injured old bear that was caught for me. When that story appeared in newspapers, a toy maker and his wife made a toy bear and named it Teddy, after me. Who am I?

Topics to explore:

▸ heroes and heroic actions

▸ landmarks

▸ historic people and events

Spotlight on Reading

Key Words

lighthouse

hero

row

lantern

rescued

drowning

tower

storms

telescope

sailboat

mast

oars

Predicting

Answer the questions in complete sentences.

1. What does the title tell you the story might be about?

2. What clues do the key words provide as to what might happen in the story?

3. Who do you think the person in the picture is? What do you think she will do in the story?

Ida Lewis to the Rescue

Written by Kathleen Muldoon

Illustrated by María Wernicke

Ida Lewis was a famous lighthouse keeper. She is a national hero because of the many lives she saved and the ships she guided to safety.

Ida was born in 1842 and lived most of her life near Newport, Rhode Island. When Ida was five, her father taught her to swim and row a boat. These were things most other girls did not do. Ida's sister teased her. She wanted Ida to stay indoors and learn to sew and cook. But Ida kept right on swimming and rowing.

Ida's father worked very hard. Every day and night, he rowed a boat from the shore at Newport to the lighthouse on Lime Rock Island. Ida went with him. Together they lit its lantern.

The lantern light shone across the water. Sailors could see it from their ships. The light told them that they were too close to rocks that could damage their ships. It also told them when they were close to land.

Mr. Lewis also saved lives. When he saw a ship in trouble, he raced to get into his boat. He often took Ida to help him. She would hold the rocking boat steady while her father rescued the drowning sailors.

When Ida was 15, her family moved to Lime Rock Island. Her father was the lighthouse keeper. The lighthouse tower was now part of their new house. Soon after moving, Ida's father became very sick and could not work. Ida's mother took care of him. Ida took charge of the lighthouse and the family.

Ida rowed to Newport every day to take her sister and brothers to school. In the afternoon, she brought them home. Twice a day, Ida checked the lantern. In the morning, she cleaned the glass and turned off the lantern. In the afternoon, she lit the lantern. She also lit it in storms to help sailors find their way.

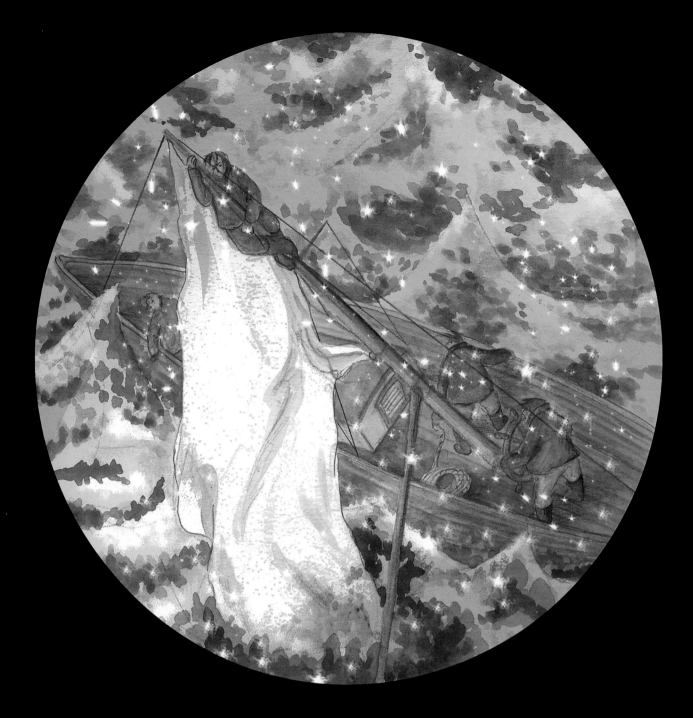

One afternoon, Ida was in front of her house,
looking at the sea with her telescope. As she looked
out across the water, she saw four boys in a sailboat.
They were laughing and pushing each other. Their
boat rocked. Then, one boy climbed the sail mast
like a monkey.

Ida gasped as she watched the sailboat turn upside down. The boys tumbled into the sea. Ida ran toward her boat.

"Don't go out!" her mother called. "It's too cold outside."

Ida did not have time to put on her boots or coat. She raced to the edge of the rock island. After pushing with all her might, she finally got the boat off the rocks and into the sea. Then she jumped in and began to row.

"Help! Help!" the boys yelled.

Cold seawater splashed onto Ida's face. Her arms ached as she pulled the oars through the icy waves. Finally, she reached the sailboat. The boys were tired from holding on to its sides. They were too tired to help Ida.

Ida was small, but she was strong. She pulled each boy into her boat. Then, she rowed back to the island. Her mother and brothers helped get the boys out of the boat. They wrapped them in blankets and gave them warm drinks. Ida was cold and wet, too. It took a while for her to get warm again.

Then, she rowed the boys back to Newport. They thanked Ida for saving their lives. But they did not tell their friends or parents what had happened. They did not want people to know that a girl had saved their lives!

After her father died, Ida became the lighthouse keeper. She saved many more people from drowning. She rescued men, women, and children. Once she saved a sheep! People in Newport called Ida a hero and surprised her by holding an Ida Lewis Day.

Ida Lewis lived on Lime Rock Island for most of her life. People in Rhode Island never forgot her. Some wrote poems about her. Sailors sang songs about her and called her the "angel of the lighthouse." Others called her the "bravest woman in America."

Checking

A Choose the correct answer.

1. When she was five years old, Ida's father taught her to …
   - a. read and write.
   - b. swim and row a boat.
   - c. rescue drowning sailors.
   - d. cook and sew.

2. Why was it important for Ida and her father to light the lantern?
   - a. The lantern warned sailors that they were too close to the shore.
   - b. The light helped villagers move around town at night.
   - c. It was a sign for ships to come closer.
   - d. The heat from the lantern kept Ida and her family warm.

3. What did Ida do for the four boys in the sailboat?
   - a. She yelled at them for being foolish.
   - b. She turned on the lantern so they could see.
   - c. She told her father to go save them.
   - d. She pulled them into her boat and rescued them.

4. How did Ida know her work was appreciated?
   - a. People sent gifts, wrote letters, and held Ida Lewis Day.
   - b. The island she lived on was renamed Ida Lewis Island.
   - c. The boys from the sailboat held a parade in her honor.
   - d. The lighthouse was closed and Ida became mayor of the town.

B Answer the Critical Thinking questions in complete sentences.

1. Why do you think Ida and her father worked so well together?

2. Do you think Ida was brave? Why or why not?

Summarizing

A   Fill in the two-column chart to make a Trait graphic organizer.

Ida Lewis

Trait	Example
strong	takes brothers and sister in rowboat

1. In the Trait column, write adjectives that describe what Ida Lewis was like.

2. Look for clues in the story that support your description of Ida.

3. Write the supporting clues in the Example column.

B   Use the information in your graphic organizer to write a summary of the story.

Reflecting

A   Discuss the following questions.

1. How did Ida Lewis become a hero?

2. What are some of the personality traits of a hero?

3. Do you need special training to be a hero? Explain your answer.

B   Imagine you are writing a book about Ida Lewis. Write sentences that describe her actions and her personality.

Spotlight on Language

Connecting

A   Listen to the description of a storm at sea.

Key Words

- bang
- claps
- crash
- hissing
- roar
- rumbles
- splashes

B   Answer the questions in complete sentences.

1. What animal hisses?

2. What animal roars?

Focusing

A Match each picture on the left with the word on the right that tells the sound the pictured object, animal, or action makes.

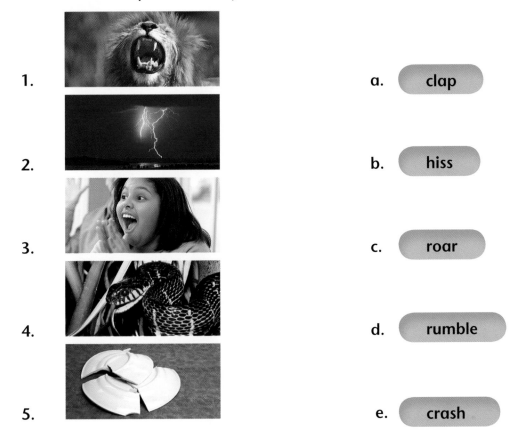

1.

2.

3.

4.

5.

a. clap

b. hiss

c. roar

d. rumble

e. crash

B Write a sentence with the words in activity A.

Applying

▶ Pretend that you are at a beach, at a party, or on a busy street. Imagine the sounds you can hear. Write a paragraph to describe all that you hear. Use words that represent sounds, such as *clap* and *roar*. Next, read the paragraph back to yourself.

Every time I walk to my house, I hear the bus roar, and it always scares me.

Connecting

Ⓐ Read and listen to the tongue twister.

She sells seashells by the seashore.
The shells she sells are surely seashells.
So if she sells shells by the seashore,
I'm sure she sells seashore shells.

Ⓑ Answer these questions in complete sentences.

1. Why do you think seashells and seashore contain the word *sea*?

2. Where would you find someone who sells fruit?

Focusing

A Which words in each sentence start with the same sound?

1. Susan sees the sea leaving seashells on the sand.

2. Sasha is scavenging the seashore for seven sumptuous seashells.

B Choose the correct word to complete each sentence about Ida Lewis.

> lighthouse   liked   stormy   inspected

1. Ida Lewis _____ living on Lime Rock Island.

2. She learned to light the lantern in the _____.

3. Invincible Ida _____ the sea incessantly.

4. She saved soldiers and sailors stranded in _____ seas.

Applying

▶ Write sentences in which most words begin with the same sound. Begin each sentence with the name of a real or imaginary person. Use words that begin with the same sound to describe what that person does.

Rachel rides the railroad to Reno.

Connecting

A Read about Ida and her father.

When Ida's father started to work as a lighthouse keeper, the Lewis family lived in Newport because the house attached to the lighthouse was not built yet. The lighthouse was about one thousand feet from Newport, so Ida's father rowed every day to get to his job. The trip didn't take long, but it was dangerous, especially in bad weather.

Ida learned to row from her father, and she became a very good rower. She also was an excellent and strong swimmer, or she would not have been able to rescue people who were drowning.

B Answer the questions in complete sentences.

1. How is the job of a lifeguard like the job of a lighthouse keeper?

2. Do you think there are lighthouse keepers today, or do you think their jobs no longer exist? Why?

Focusing

A In each numbered item, find the word that connects the two sentences. Then, rewrite the sentence as two separate sentences.

1. In the 1800s, there were no electric lights, so people used oil lanterns to have light at night.

2. The house on Lime Rock Island is still there, but now it's a private yacht club.

3. Ida Lewis was a hero because she saved many people.

4. You can read a book about Ida Lewis, or you can look her up on the Internet.

B Use the words in the box to connect the two sentences.

> so   because   but

1. Yesterday we didn't go to school. There was a snowstorm.

2. It is known that Ida rescued 18 persons who were drowning. Many people believe she rescued more.

3. It's easy to fall off a boat. You should always wear a life jackets.

Applying

▶ Imagine that you went to work with a family member. Write about what you did together and about something the family member taught you to do. Connect sentences with words such as *and*, *but*, and *so*.

My father is a baker, and today he took me to work at five in the morning with him ...

Personal Journal Entry

August 27

Today was an amazing day! My family and I went to Mount Rushmore National Monument, which is in South Dakota. The mountain has the faces of four presidents carved into its side. It took 14 years to finish!

Looking up at the stone faces was really great! My dad told me that Abraham Lincoln was born in a log cabin, and his family was ver poor. It made me think about how people in this country are lucky to have so many opportunities. I wond who the next heroes will be.

▶ Answer the questions about the text in complete sentences.

1. Why do you think the text starts with a date?

2. Why does it look like it's written in a book?

3. Whose experiences does the author write about?

Writing a Personal Journal Entry

A personal journal is a way of keeping a record of your life. Journal entries always start with a date. They are descriptions of what you, the author, did that day. They also include your personal opinions and feelings about the events of the day. Occasionally, you can draw sketches to illustrate something you write about.

Tips for writing a personal journal:

- A journal entry is usually about what you experience during one day.

- Instead of just telling what you did, also write about your personal thoughts and feelings.

- Since you are writing about things that happened before, be sure you use verbs in the past tense.

- For clarity, your paragraphs should follow a logical or sequential order.

▶ Write a personal journal entry.

1. In the first paragraph, write about what happened to you that day.

2. In the second paragraph, go into more detail about the most interesting things that happened.

3. In the third and fourth paragraphs, talk about your own personal thoughts and feelings. How did what happened that day affect you?

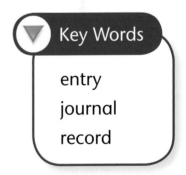

▼ Key Words

entry

journal

record

Parts of a Book

Books are divided into parts or sections. Some parts appear at the beginning, in the main part of the book, or at the end.

Parts at the beginning

- The title page is the first page with text on it. It includes the title, the author's name, the publisher's name, and the city where the book was published.
- The table of contents is an outline for the book. It includes the names of the sections and chapters and the page numbers where these begin. The table of contents lists items in numerical order.

Main part

The main part of the book is called the body. The body of the book is usually divided into chapters or units. Each of these sections has its own title. It tells you what the subject, or theme, of the chapter or unit is.

Parts at the end

- The glossary explains words that are used in the text. You can use it to look up the meanings of words. The words appear in alphabetical order.
- Some books include a bibliography. This is a list of books, articles, and Internet sites about the subject of the book. If you want to know more about a subject, you can check the bibliography for other sources.
- The index is the last part of the book.
  It is a list of the topics that are in the book.
  The topics are listed in alphabetical order.
  Each topic is followed by the page number
  on which it appears in the body of the book.

Key Words

bibliography
body
glossary
index
table of contents
title page

▶ Answer the questions in complete sentences.

1. What information do you find on the title page of this book?

2. On what page does the glossary begin?

3. How are the words in the glossary listed?

4. How many pages is the table of contents?

5. What do the numbers in the index represent?

6. How many units are in this book?

7. Is there a bibliography in this book?

8. On what page does the index begin?

Revising

Ⓐ Review the personal journal entry you wrote to complete the activity on page 233.

- What day did you choose to write about? Why did you choose it?

- Did you focus your writing on the most interesting parts of your experience?

- Did you remember to include personal details in your journal entry?

- Are the verbs in the past tense?

- Did you use proper punctuation and capitalization?

Ⓑ Rewrite your personal journal entry, making any necessary corrections.

Weight

Weight is a measure of how heavy an object, a person, or an animal is. Weight changes according to gravity, which is the force that pulls you to Earth. In space there is zero gravity, so objects, people, and animals have no weight there.

The ounce and the pound are standard units of weight in the United States. The abbreviations for ounce and pound are not shortened forms of the English words but of their linguistic origins. The abbreviation for ounce is "oz," which is short for the old Italian word *onza*. The abbreviation for pound is "lb," which is short for the Latin word *libra*.

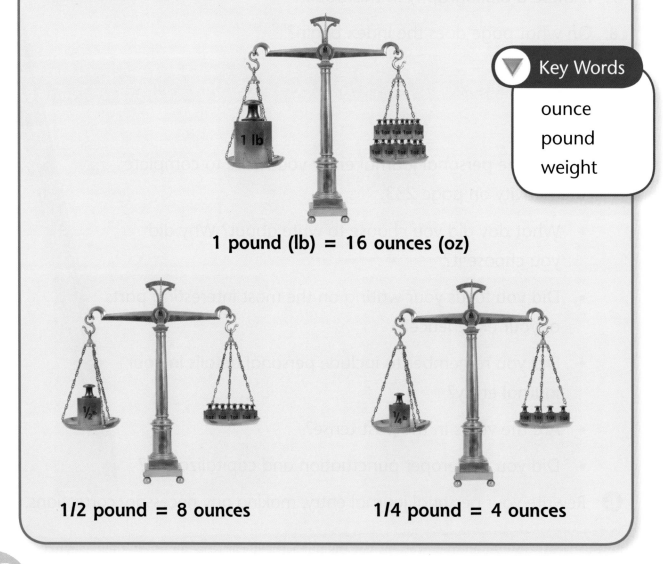

1 pound (lb) = 16 ounces (oz)

> **Key Words**
>
> ounce
> pound
> weight

1/2 pound = 8 ounces

1/4 pound = 4 ounces

A Predict whether the first item in each pair weighs less, more, or about the same as the second item.

B Determine what you think are the lightest and heaviest items in your backpack. Would you use ounces or pounds to tell the weight of each item? Why?

C Answer the questions in complete sentences.

1. If one item weighs two pounds, and another item weighs thirty-three ounces, how would you determine which one is heavier?

2. How would you determine how many quarter-pound hamburgers you could make out of three pounds of ground beef?

3. How would you determine how many ounces are in six pounds? Write your answer as a number sentence.

Navigation Aids

Lighthouses still guide to shore all kinds of ships and boats. Many lighthouses are at the entrance to harbors and bays. They are very useful at night and in bad weather. They warn sailors of dangers.

The earliest known lighthouse was on the island of Pharos, off the coast of Egypt. It was built more than 2,000 years ago. It produced light by burning wood at the top of its tower.

Fire was still the source of light during the time Ida Lewis lived. Keepers burned whale oil and other fuels in special lanterns. They had to light the lantern each night, make sure it stayed lit through the night, and turn it off in the morning, Through the use of mirrors and special lenses, the brightness of the light was increased.

Lighthouses were also used as landmarks. They were painted in different color patterns for identification. Ship captains could then tell their location when they spotted a particular lighthouse.

Today technological advances such as radar and the global positioning system (GPS) can show the exact location of a ship, no matter where it is. The global positioning system is based on satellites that orbit, or circle, the earth. Many lighthouses are no longer used, but the lighthouse keepers who saved lives and became heroes will never be forgotten.

This lighthouse on the coast of New Jersey has been operating for over 300 years. It is one of the oldest lighthouses in the United States.

This is one of the NAVSTAR satellites that make possible the operation of the Global Positioning System, or GPS.

A Read the sentences and decide whether they refer to the duties of a lighthouse keeper or of a ship's captain.

1. Light the lantern for the night.

2. Identify a lighthouse.

3. Find out where the ship is.

4. Make sure you can see light coming from the lighthouse.

B Research lighthouses.

1. On a map of the United States, locate the states on the East and West Coasts. Choose a state and draw its outline.

2. Research whether the state of your choice has lighthouses. Mark their location on the outline map you drew.

3. Present your map to the class. Point out the harbors and bays in which the lighthouses are located.

C Compare and contrast how lighthouses and global-positioning-system devices help sailors navigate.

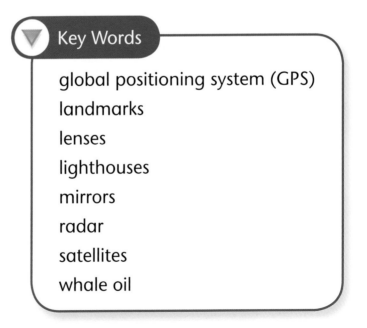

Key Words

global positioning system (GPS)
landmarks
lenses
lighthouses
mirrors
radar
satellites
whale oil

Light

Light is a form of energy. Natural light comes from sources like the sun and fire. Artificial, or man-made, light comes from sources like lightbulbs.

Light has very special properties:

- Light travels in a straight line, moving very fast.

- Light can pass through objects that are transparent, such as clear glass. Some light can pass through objects that are translucent, such as frosted glass. Light cannot pass through objects that are opaque, such as a piece of cardboard.

- Shadows form when opaque objects block the passing of light.

- Light reflects, or bounces back, when it strikes a smooth, shiny surface, such as a mirror. It refracts, or bends, when it passes through glass or water.

Lenses are pieces of glass that can direct and control light. Depending on their shape, lenses can make light stronger. A lens' surface can be convex (when the lens is rounded outward) or concave (when it is rounded inward). Lenses and mirrors have many uses. They are used in cameras, microscopes, telescopes, and other instruments.

Key Words

concave
convex
lenses
light
opaque
reflects
refracts
translucent
transparent

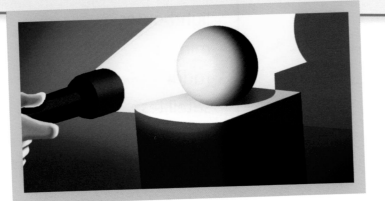

Science

A Choose the correct word to complete each sentence according to the reading.

| concave | lenses | opaque |
| reflects | refracted | transparent |

1. If an object is clear, it is _____.

2. When light bounces off a smooth object, it _____.

3. The surface of a _____ lens is like the inside of a bowl.

4. When light bends through water, it is _____.

5. If something is _____, light cannot pass through it.

6. Eyeglasses are an example of how _____ are useful.

B Think of as many sources of light as you can. Write them down in a two-column chart, according to whether they are natural or artificial.

C Experiment with bending light. Fill a clear plastic glass halfway with water. Place a pencil in the glass and observe what happens under different conditions.

1. Describe what you observe if you hold the pencil straight in the water.

2. Describe what you observe if you let the pencil rest against the side of the glass.

3. Describe what you observe if you add more water to the glass.

4. Write your observations in your notebook.

Sing Along

A Listen to the song.

America the Beautiful

O beautiful for spacious skies,
For amber waves of grain,
For purple mountain majesties
Above the fruited plain!

America! America!
God shed His grace on thee,
And crown thy good
With brotherhood
From sea to shining sea!

O beautiful for patriot dream
That sees beyond the years,
Thine alabaster cities gleam
Undimmed by human tears!

America! America!
God shed His grace on thee,
And crown thy good
With brotherhood,
From sea to shining sea!

B Sing the song.

C Answer the questions in complete sentences.

1. What words are used to describe the places mentioned in the song?

2. What word could you use in place of each highlighted word in the song?

FROM EAST TO WEST

Written by Anastasia Suen

Photo selection by Mónica Delgado de Patrucco

The first immigrants to this country settled near the Atlantic Ocean. Over the years, more people came and moved farther west. The country grew. Soon it reached all the way to the Pacific Ocean. Because it was so big, it took a long time to travel from one side to the other.

The families that moved west often traveled in wagons.
Oxen and horses pulled the wagons, so they moved very
slowly. It took months to get from one end of the country to
the other. People started their journey in early spring. They
traveled through summer and fall. If they kept walking,
they could reach the west coast before winter. Once the snow
came, it was very hard to travel.

There were no trains across the country. President Lincoln wanted railroads to reach from east to west. In 1862, he signed the Pacific Railroad Act. Two railroad companies began to build a railroad line from California to Nebraska. The Central Pacific Railroad started in California. The Union Pacific Railroad started in Nebraska. They built toward each other and met in the middle.

Many of the railroad workers came from the gold mines in California. These men went to California to find gold. They didn't find any gold, so they worked for the railroad instead. The railroad hired many Chinese workers. Some Chinese workers came to find gold. Others left China because of famine. The railroad company even sent a man to China to find more workers for the railroad.

The Central Pacific Railroad had to cross the mountains. The mountains were steep and rocky. The workers had to use explosives to break the rocks. It was very dangerous work, and many workers died. The winter weather was also a problem. There was so much snow, it was difficult to work. It was hard to see when there were blizzards. Avalanches buried men alive. Still, the work on the railroad went on.

The Union Pacific Railroad started in Omaha, Nebraska. Many of the workers were veterans of the Civil War. Old soldiers from the North and the South came to work for the railroad. Some of them wore their old uniforms. But they weren't fighting each other anymore. Now they were working together. Workers from Ireland also helped build the railroad. They left Ireland because of famine and came to America to start a new life. When they couldn't find jobs in the city, they came to work on the railroad.

The Union Pacific Railroad had to cross the plains. They needed wood to build the railroad. There weren't enough trees there, and the few trees that did grow there weren't strong enough. They had to bring supplies from far away. The weather was also a problem. It was hard to work in the heavy rains. One spring, the rains even washed away the bridges! They had to build them all over again.

Some of the Native Americans that lived on the plains didn't like the railroad. They didn't want it to cross their lands. Other Native Americans, however, were hired to work on the railroad. Some of them were hired to guard the tracks from attacks.

After years of work, the two railroads finally reached each other. The tracks of the Central Pacific Railroad joined the tracks of the Union Pacific Railroad at Promontory Point, Utah. On May 10, 1869, the railroad owners hammered in the last spike. It was a special, golden spike. Workers from both railroads came to see. Then, a train from each side moved forward and touched. The workers put up telegraph lines as they were building the railroad. When the last spike was hammered in, a telegraph worker spelled out the word "Done!"

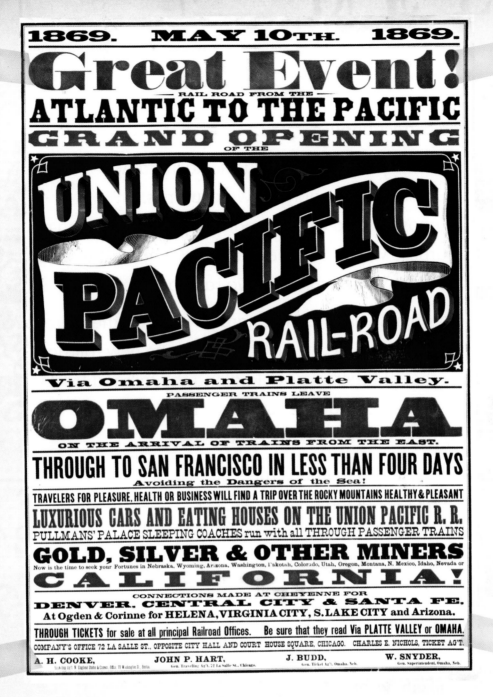

The message was sent all over the country along the new telegraph lines. When the news came, people in cities and towns rang bells. In New York City, the Navy fired off a 200-gun salute. After a big celebration, the railroads went to work. Trains carried passengers from east to west. At last, people could travel by rail across the entire continent. The transcontinental railroad was complete. A person could travel from one end of the country to the other in just a week. What used to take months could be done in days!

Checking

A Choose the correct answer.

1. What was the purpose of the Pacific Railroad Act?
   a. Its purpose was to connect two countries.
   b. Its purpose was to create separate railroad companies.
   c. Its purpose was to help people travel from east to west.
   d. Its purpose was to connect two railroad companies.

2. Why did Chinese and Irish immigrants work on the railroad?
   a. They wanted to be the first to ride on the new railroad.
   b. They thought there was gold along the railroad tracks.
   c. They came from families who had no food.
   d. They thought the work was very easy.

3. Where did the two railroads meet?
   a. They met in Sacramento, California.
   b. They met in Omaha, Nebraska.
   c. They met at Promontory Point, Utah.
   d. They met in Chicago, Illinois.

4. How long did it take to cross the country on the new railroad?
   a. It took one day.
   b. It took one week.
   c. It took one month.
   d. It took several months, from spring to fall.

B Answer the Critical Thinking questions in complete sentences.

1. Why was it better for people to use the railroad than to travel in covered wagons?

2. Why do you think some Native Americans didn't like the railroad?

3. Why do you think the last spike was made out of gold?

Summarizing

A Fill in the Sequence graphic organizer.

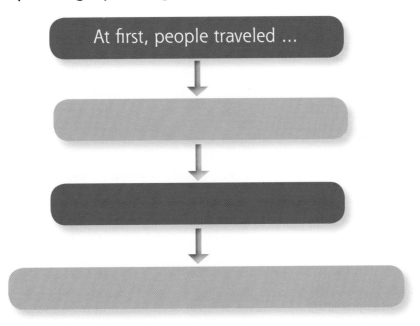

At first, people traveled …

1. In the first box, write how people traveled at the beginning of the story.

2. In the second box, write what had to be done to allow people to travel faster.

3. In the third box, write what was built and how it was accomplished.

4. In the fourth box, write how people traveled at the end of the story.

B When you finish, use the information in your graphic organizer to write a summary of the story.

Reflecting

▶ Write a short essay that compares and contrasts traveling from east to west before and after the transcontinental railroad was built.

Spotlight on Language

Connecting

A   Listen to a tour guide talk to visitors at the site where the railroads met.

Key Words

airline
airplane
locomotive
reenactment
replicas

B   Answer the questions in complete sentences.

1. What sorts of replicas might you find in your home?

2. If you went to a Civil War reenactment, what might you see there?

3. Why do you think the word *locomotive* is not used anymore? What word do we use in its place?

Focusing

A Choose the right word to complete each pair of sentences.

1. (paint/painted)
   a. Airlines _____ their airplanes.
   b. In the 1800s, railroad companies _____ their locomotives.

2. (own/owned)
   a. When the automobile was invented, only the very rich _____ them.
   b. Today most families _____ at least one car.

3. (burn/burned)
   a. In modern times, trains _____ diesel instead of coal.
   b. In the 1800s and early 1900s, trains _____ coal.

B Choose the correct word from the box to complete each sentence.

met   did   brought   was

1. He _____ most of the work himself.

2. I _____ my best friend at camp last summer.

3. My aunt _____ me a pie when she came to visit.

4. Mrs. Jackson _____ my teacher last year.

Applying

▶ Write a short essay about a visit you made to a place where you learned about something important that happened in the past. Remember to include where you went and when, what you did, and what you learned.

Last summer I went to Hawaii to visit ...

Connecting

A Listen and read about how trains have changed.

The first trains were pulled by steam locomotives. A steam locomotive burns coal to heat a boiler filled with water. The water changes to steam. The force of the steam pushes a piston that makes the wheels of the locomotive turn.

The steam locomotive was invented in England by Richard Trevithick. The fastest his first locomotive could go was five miles per hour. Over time, steam locomotives improved and became much faster.

Today diesel locomotives pull most trains. Diesel is a fuel like gasoline. Diesel trains can travel up to 100 miles per hour. They carry passengers and cargo all over the country.

Some electric trains are even faster. These are called high-speed trains. They can reach a speed of 180 miles per hour. That is about three times as fast as a car on a highway. High-speed trains travel between major cities. In the United States, there is a high-speed train that travels in the Northeast, between Washington DC and Boston.

Train pulled by a steam locomotive.

Train pulled by a diesel locomotive.

Train pulled by an electric locomotive.

B Answer the questions in complete sentences.

1. What fuel is used to heat your home?

2. What fuel is used to make cars run?

3. What are trains used for today?

Focusing

A Use *is* or *are* to complete the following sentences.

1. Traveling by train _____ a great way to see the countryside.

2. There _____ a museum at Promontory Point, where the two train tracks connected.

3. Telegrams, like steam locomotives, _____ not used very much anymore.

4. Richard Trevithick _____ famous for being the inventor of the locomotive.

5. Electric locomotives _____ faster than steam locomotives.

B Choose the correct word from the box to complete each sentence.

heat   changes   makes   go   carry

1. If you don't want to drive, traveling by train is a good way to _____.

2. The engine _____ the train move.

3. Some trains _____ only cargo.

4. _____ the water to boil it.

5. The liquid _____ to a gas.

Applying

▶ imagine you are riding on one of the trains pictured on page 262. Write a paragraph to describe the ride: *Is the ride noisy? How fast is the train moving? ...*

I am riding on the train pulled by a ...

Connecting

A   Read about the plans for a summer train trip.

I can't wait for summer vacation to begin. This year it will be special. My parents, my grandfather, my older sister, and I will travel from our home in Chicago all the way to Los Angeles. There we will stay at my aunt Elizabeth's home. I haven't seen my cousins in a very long time.

We will ride the train for almost two entire days. It's going to be a long ride, but there will be lots of things to see along the way. The train will cross the Mississippi River. We will go across the mountains of New Mexico, and we will go through a tunnel that is a half-mile long! We will see farms that grow wheat, ranches with cows and horses, and deserts where few people live. We will stop in Flagstaff, which is right next to the Grand Canyon in Arizona.

On the train, there will be movies to watch, and we will take board games to play. I also will take a diary, and I will write about what I see and do every day.

B   Answer the questions in complete sentences.

1. Why do few people live in deserts?

2. What is the difference between a farm and a ranch?

3. How could you build a tunnel through a mountain?

Focusing

▶ Rewrite the sentences to show that the action will happen at a future time.

1. We travel in the summer.

2. I write in my notebook.

3. Our family stays with my aunt Elizabeth.

4. I ride on the train.

5. We also stop in Arizona.

6. My sister and I take board games to play.

7. We see farms along the way.

8. Together on the train we cross hundreds of miles.

Applying

▶ Write a paragraph about activities that you and other people will do during the summer.

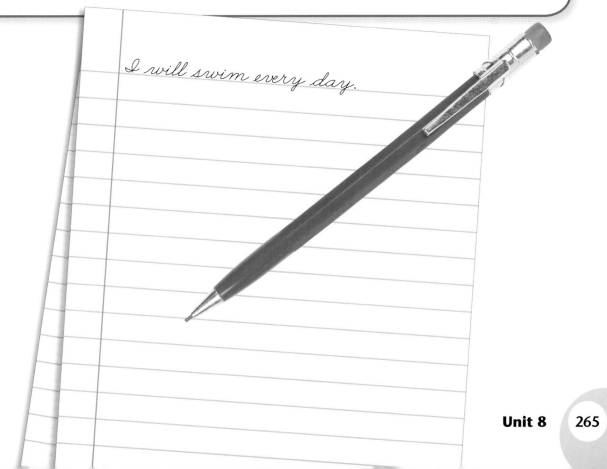

I will swim every day.

Personal Narrative

Moving Across the Country

Moving across the country is a lot of work! After the movers took everything we packed, my mom had to figure out what roads to take and where to stay, because we were doing our move by car.

We left the day after I finished the school year. I said good-bye to my friends and then, got into the car. It was really crowded in the car because we had a lot of boxes with us. The first night was fun, because we stayed in a hotel. It even had a swimming pool!

My favorite part of the trip was when we saw the Grand Canyon. The Grand Canyon is in Arizona. It is really pretty. If you want, you can ride down to the bottom of it on a mule! I wanted to try it, but we still had a long way to go. Mom said the next time we go, when I'm older, I can try it.

After five days of riding in the car, I was ready for the trip to end. I liked staying in hotels and seeing all the different parts of America. But sometimes it seemed as if we were never going to get to our destination. When we finally got to our new house, the boxes with our things weren't there yet. So the first night, we slept on the floor. I wished I was back in a hotel! Our things arrived the next day, and everything was good after that.

▶ Answer the questions in complete sentences.

1. In this story, does the author write about a character or about himself or herself?

2. Do you think this story actually happened? Why or why not?

Writing a Personal Narrative

A narrative is a piece of writing that tells a story. It can be a story about a personal experience. To write a personal narrative, think of experiences in your life that you will always remember, such as winning a prize, welcoming a baby brother or sister, or moving to another country. List events in the order in which they happened. Remember to use the past tense. Describe how you felt as the events were taking place.

Tips for writing a personal narrative:

• Describe when and where the experience you describe took place.

• Describe who was involved and what happened.

• Make it more interesting by including unexpected, funny, or scary moments.

▶ Write a personal narrative that describes a special experience in your life.

1. In the first paragraph, introduce what the narrative is about in a way that will interest the reader.

2. In the second paragraph, start writing about your experience in the order that it happened.

3. In the third paragraph, write about something that was especially interesting.

4. In the fourth paragraph, write a conclusion summarizing what happened and how you felt about it.

Key Words

events

experience

narrative

order

when

where

who

Review: Subject-Verb Agreement

Remember that a sentence has two main parts: the subject and the predicate. The subject is who the sentence is about. It can be singular or plural. Singular means one, and plural means more than one. The predicate is the part of the sentence that contains the verb. The verb should always agree with the subject in number and in form.

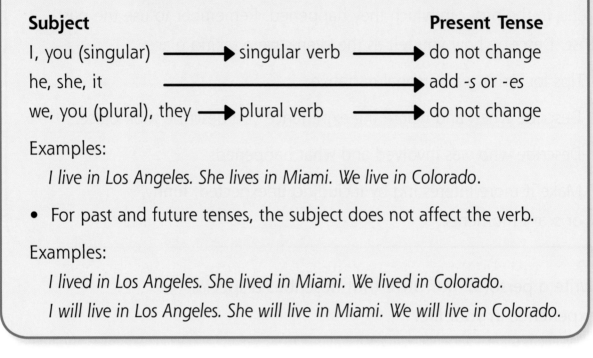

Examples:

I live in Los Angeles. She lives in Miami. We live in Colorado.

• For past and future tenses, the subject does not affect the verb.

Examples:

I lived in Los Angeles. She lived in Miami. We lived in Colorado.

I will live in Los Angeles. She will live in Miami. We will live in Colorado.

A Complete each sentence with the verb in parentheses. If needed, add the suffix -s or -es to the verb.

1. Now my father _____ the train to and from work every day. (ride)

2. As soon as we got to the new house, I wanted to _____. (unpack)

3. The new house _____ smaller than the old one. (look)

4. Our new neighbor _____ to us whenever she sees us. (wave)

B Change the subject of each sentence to its singular form. Then, rewrite the sentences.

Key Words

agree
plural
predicate
singular
subject
verb

1. They play tennis every day.

2. We walked to the park.

3. We were late.

4. You all help build America.

Revising

A Review the personal narrative you wrote to complete the activity on page 267.

- **Did** you make sure to write about the most interesting parts of your experience, how you felt, and your thoughts?

- **What** verbs did you use? Are they in the past tense? Do they agree with the subject?

- **Did** you use words like *first*, *next*, and *finally* so the reader knows the order in which things happened?

B Rewrite your personal narrative, making any necessary corrections.

Place Value and Expanded Notation

A digit is any of the ten symbols we use to write numbers:

0   1   2   3   4   5   6   7   8   9

Place value refers to the value of a digit according to its place, or position, in a number. For example:

1 in the ones position = 1 (one)

1 in the thousands position = 1,000 (one thousand)

1 in the millions position = 1,000,000 (one million)

millions	hundred thousands	ten thousands	thousands	hundreds	tens	ones
						1
			1	0	0	0
1	0	0	0	0	0	0

Notice that, beginning with one thousand, a comma is used to separate numbers into groups of three.

Numbers are usually written using the digits 0–9. This form of writing numbers is called standard notation.

Another way to write numbers is by showing the place value of its digits. This form of writing numbers is called expanded notation. This is a longer way of writing the same number.

Standard notation: 9,346

Expanded notation: 9000 + 300 + 40 + 6

A Read each number aloud from the table.

numbers	thousands	hundreds	tens	ones
791				
8,288				
17,295				

1. Copy and complete the table.

2. Rewrite the numbers in expanded notation.

B For each of the following numbers, tell what place the number nine is in.

1. 9,366,433
2. 1,294
3. 459
4. 2,936
5. 593,182
6. 9,157

C Tell how you would solve each problem. Then, write the number sentences you would use to solve them.

1. On the wagon trail, five families were traveling together. Each family consisted of three adults and two children. How many people were traveling together?

2. A train going to Sacramento, California, had four passenger cars. Two cars had 20 passengers each. The other two cars had 30 passengers each. How many passengers were traveling on the train?

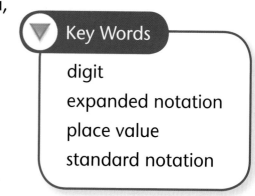

Key Words

digit

expanded notation

place value

standard notation

Native Americans

Native Americans were the first people to live on the land that has become the United States. They lived in different groups called tribes. Each tribe developed its own culture, language, customs, and way of life. Shelter, food, and the activities varied among the tribes, depending on what each group had in its environment.

In the Southwest, for example, the Hopi and other Pueblo tribes lived in homes made of adobe, a local clay that they shaped into bricks and dried in the sun. The homes were built in groups on the sides of hills. They also used the clay to make beautiful pottery. Even though they lived in the desert, they were excellent farmers. They grew a special kind of corn that didn't need much water.

Native Americans who lived in the Great Plains, between the Rocky Mountains and the Mississippi River, were excellent hunters. They hunted buffalo. The buffalo fulfilled several basic needs. The Indians used its meat for food and its bones to make tools. And they used its hide to make clothes and covers for their homes, called teepees. Teepees were like modern tents. The Plains tribes were nomads. They moved from place to place, taking the teepees with them.

There were many other groups of Native Americans living in the land that has become the United States. In middle of the 1800s, as settlers moved west, they began to put up fences in the open fields. These were the Native Americans' farming and hunting grounds. In the end, the United States government moved the Native Americans from their lands. They were sent to special areas, called reservations.

A Match each term with its definition.

1. adobe

a. area of land set up by the government for Native Americans to live on

2. Great Plains

b. house made of buffalo hides, similar to a tent

3. nomads

c. sun-dried brick made of clay

4. reservations

d. a person who moves from place to place

5. teepee

e. flat, grassy land between the Rocky Mountains and the Mississippi River

B Answer the questions with the name of the correct tribe.

1. Who used adobe to build their homes?

2. Who lived in teepees?

3. Who were excellent potters?

4. Who were excellent hunters?

C Research one of the Native American tribes mentioned in the reading.

1. Write a short description of that tribe.

2. Describe their interactions with the new settlers.

Key Words

adobe
buffalo
Great Plains
Hopi
nomads
Pueblo
reservations
Southwest
teepees
tribes

Communication Technology

Throughout history, we have had the need to communicate news, information, and personal messages. How do we send these messages? Methods of communication have evolved over time, from using natural objects to inventing man-made objects. These new technologies make communication faster and easier.

In ancient times, some cultures had human messengers. Some Native Americans communicated with smoke signals to warn others of danger. Some other cultures used conch shells or ram horns to produce sounds to send messages. People, fire, conch shells, and ram horns are natural objects.

We have changed the way we communicate through the use of man-made objects and the development of new technologies. Samuel Morse invented the telegraph to send and receive written messages called telegrams. Morse developed a code of dots and dashes that stood for letters. The coded messages traveled over man-made electrical wires. Next, Alexander Graham Bell invented the telephone, which carried voice messages over electrical wires. Today you can talk to anybody from almost anywhere with a cell phone. A cell phone does not need to be connected to an electrical line.

Using natural objects for communication is no longer necessary, thanks to the inventions that have advanced communication technology.

Key Words

cell phone
human messengers
smoke signals
telegrams
telegraph
telephone

A Imagine that you worked as a telegraph operator in the late 1800s. Write a two-sentence news message, and convert it to Morse Code using the chart below.

The Morse Code

A	B	C	D	E	F
G	H	I	J	K	L
M	N	O	P	Q	R
S	T	U	V	W	X
Y	Z				

B Select one of the man-made objects mentioned in the text. Research how it works. Write a detailed explanation and present it to the class. Be sure to include visual aids in your presentation.

Sing Along

A Listen to the song.

I've been workin' on the railroad,
All the live long day.
I've been workin' on the railroad,
Just to pass the time away.
Don't you hear the whistle blowing?
Rise up so early in the morn.
Don't you hear the captain shouting,
"Dinah, blow your horn?"

Dinah, won't you blow,
Dinah, won't you blow,
Dinah, won't you blow your horn?
Dinah, won't you blow,
Dinah, won't you blow,
Dinah, won't you blow your horn?

B Sing the song.

C Answer the questions in complete sentences.

1. Who or what is Dinah? What might the horn and whistle be for?

2. What are some other words for *railroad*?

3. What might the job of the captain be?

The Statue of Liberty

How do you make drawings to represent words that stand for ideas, such as freedom? Some artists have found an answer to this question by creating what is called an allegory. An allegory is a painting or a sculpture that represents an idea.

The Statue of Liberty is an allegory that represents freedom, or liberty. Freedom is represented in the form of a woman holding a torch. Some people call her "Lady Liberty."

The statue, dedicated in 1886, was a gift from the French people to the American people, in celebration of the one-hundredth anniversary of American independence (1776). The French sculptor Frédéric-Auguste Bartholdi created this world-famous monument.

A Create an allegory.

1. Think about the word *strength*. List objects or animals with which you would associate the word *strength*.

2. Decide on an image that you think would represent the word.

3. Draw and color that image on a large sheet of paper.

Supplies

- white art paper
- pencil and eraser
- crayons or colored pencils

B Write about your allegory.

1. Write a paragraph that describes how or why your drawing represents the concept of strength.

2. Discuss the symbolism of your allegory in comparison with the symbolism of the Statue of Liberty.

Impressions

Celebrating Thanksgiving

The first Thanksgiving holiday meal in the United States was in 1621. The Wampanoag Indians and the Pilgrims joined together in Plymouth, Massachusetts, to give thanks for a plentiful harvest.

Today Thanksgiving is an American holiday celebrated in November. The traditional family meal includes turkey, mashed potatoes, vegetables, and pumpkin pie.

A   Answer the following questions.

  1. What is Thanksgiving?

  2. How is it celebrated?

B   Discuss the similarities and differences between Thanksgiving and a celebration from your family's country of origin.

Your Personal Narrative

▶ Write a personal narrative about a special experience you have had during this school year. Include the following:

- A description of the experience.
- What the experience meant to you at the time.
- What you think of the experience now.
- How you will remember the experience in the future.

The Writing Process

Remember, the writing process includes a series of steps:

- **Developing Ideas** Use the Internet, visual elements, or other references to help you gather and develop ideas.

- **Organizing** Choose the ideas you want to use. Put them in order, connect them, or discard the least important ones.

- **Drafting** Use the ideas you organized to write paragraphs.

- **Revising** Read your paragraphs again and correct your writing, keeping in mind what you learned in this unit.

- **Rewriting** Produce a clean copy of your piece, applying all the corrections, to display in class.

Remember, you can always repeat a step if you need to.

A

abundance *n.,* a great amount

action verbs *n.,* words that tell that someone or something is doing something

addition *n.,* a math operation indicated by the plus sign

adjective *n.,* a word that modifies a noun

adobe *n.,* a sun-dried brick made of clay and straw

adventure *n.,* an experience that is new and exciting

adverb *n.,* a word that modifies a verb

agree *v.,* to match in number, gender, person, or tense

airplane *n.,* machine that flies in the air

Amir *n.,* main character in *Amir's New School*

and *conj.,* a word meaning *also* that is used to connect other words, phrases, and clauses

ant *n.,* an insect that lives in tunnels in the ground

are *v.,* the third-person, plural, present-tense of the verb *to be*

area *n.,* the length inside a shape or the space it takes up

article *n.,* an individual piece of writing that is part of a newspaper or magazine

ate *v.,* took into the mouth as food

auditorium *n.,* a large room used for performances

aunts *n.,* the sisters of one's mother or father

avalanche *n.,* the sudden fall of material, such as snow or ice, down the side of a mountain

B

backpack *n.,* a school supply used to carry books and other school supplies to and from school

bait *n.,* an object used on a hook or in a trap to catch fish, birds, or other animals

bang *n.,* a sudden loud noise

basketball *n.,* a round, inflated ball used to play the sport of basketball

bathroom *n.,* a room that usually has a sink, toilet, and a bathtub or shower

bay *n.,* a body of water, partially enclosed by land

beans *n.,* seeds or pods of various plants that are eaten as vegetables

because *conj.,* since; for the reason that

becomes *v.*, comes to be; or grows into

begins *v.*, takes the first step in doing something

bibliography *n.*, a list of books, articles, and Internet sites used as source materials

big *adj.*, of a large size, weight, height, or amount

bills *n.*, legal paper money

black *adj.*, very dark (color)

blizzard *n.*, a powerful snowstorm with strong winds

blue jeans *n.*, trousers made of denim fabric

body *n.*, the main part of a book, article, or letter

book *n.*, printed or written pages bound within covers

borrow *v.*, to get something on loan and promise to return it

bowl *n.*, deep dish used for holding foods or liquids

braid *n.*, something formed by interweaving three or more strands

braiding *v.*, interweaving three or more strands of something to form a braid

bread crumbs *n.*, small pieces of bread

bridges *n.*, structures that connect two parts of land to allow easier crossing from one to the other

brought *v.*, carried or invited with

buddy *n.*, a partner with whom a student is paired to perform a task

bucket *n.*, deep, round, hollow container used to carry things

buffalo *n.*, large, wild, oxlike animal such as a bison

bull *n.*, adult male animal in the bovine family

burned *v.*, destroyed by fire

but *conj.*, on the contrary; rather

buy *v.*, to purchase with money

by *prep.*, next to; near

C

cabinet *n.*, the people appointed to work with the U.S. president

cafeteria *n.*, a school location where students eat lunch

cafeteria worker *n.*, a school worker who prepares and serves lunch

can absorb *v.*, able to soak up

can bathe *v.*, able to give a bath

can do *v.*, able to do something

can go *v.*, able to move

can help *v.*, able to give assistance to

can move *v.*, able to change position

can pull *v.*, able to apply force to bring something toward you

can't *v.*, not able; contraction of *cannot*

capital *n.*, town or city that is the official center of government

carefully *adv.*, with care or attention

cat *n.*, small domestic animal in the feline family

cell phone *n.*, portable telephone that transmits sound through the air, rather than through telephone lines

cents *n.*, parts of a dollar, usually coins, written as decimals to the hundredth place

centimeter *n.*, one hundredth of a meter

characteristics *n.*, distinguishing features or qualities

cities *n.*, large, important towns

cityscape *n.*, a painting or photograph that represents a city

claps *n.*, sudden loud sounds, usually used to describe the sounds made by thunder or hands

classify *v.*, to arrange or divide by classes or groups

classroom *n.*, a school location where students meet with their teacher for instruction

closing *n.*, the end or conclusion of something

coins *n.*, small pieces of metal authorized for use as money

cold-blooded *adj.*, having a body temperature that matches the environment

comma *n.*, a punctuation mark that separates ideas in sentences

community *n.*, a group of people who live in the same town under the same government

computer lab *n.*, a room used for computer work or research

conclusion *n.*, what a scientist decides after testing an idea

condition *n.*, state of being

condor *n.*, large bird with a wingspan of about ten feet

conserve *v.*, to save or use natural resources wisely

cornucopia *n.*, a horn overflowing with food that is used as a symbol of abundance

cousins *n.*, the sons or daughters of an aunt or uncle

crash *v.*, to make a loud clattering noise as the result of an impact

creatures *n.*, living beings, such as animals or humans

crescent *adj.*, a quarter of a sphere, meeting at a point at both ends, with a thicker center

crescent moon *n.*, the phase of the moon shape can be seen

crossing guard *n.*, a school worker who stops traffic so students can cross the street

cupcake *n.*, a small, individual cake baked in a cup-shaped mold

curly *adj.*, having a spiral or curvy appearance

custodian *n.*, a school worker who keeps the school clean

D

decimeter *n.*, one tenth of a meter

declarative *adj.*, serving to state or declare

demand *n.*, an urgent need or requirement

description *n.*, a statement or account that describes

descriptive words *n.*, words that describe, such as adjectives and adverbs

desert *n.*, a dry, sandy area with little rain and few plants

details *n.*, examples or descriptions that help us to talk about an idea

did *v.*, accomplished or performed; past tense of *to do*

didn't *v.*, contraction of *did not*

difference *n.*, the result of a subtraction operation

digestion *n.*, the process of eating and swallowing food

digit *n.*, any of the ten symbols (0–9) used to write numbers

dime *n.*, a U.S. coin worth ten cents

directions *n.*, the words used to provide instruction or guidance

disagree *v.*, to fail to agree

display *n.*, a public exhibition or show

distance *n.*, the amount of space between two things

dividing *v.*, separating into equal parts

division *n.*, the math operation used to find out how many times one quantity can be equally divided into smaller quantities

divisor *n.*, a number by which another number is divided

doesn't *v.*, contraction of *does not*

dollars *n.*, coins or notes worth one hundred cents each

don't *v.*, contraction of *do not*

dreamed *v.*, imagined while sleeping

drive *v.*, to travel by vehicle

drown *v.*, to inhale water and suffocate

E

early *adv.*, before the expected or usual time

ears *n.*, the parts of body used for hearing

earthworm *n.*, a long slender animal with no backbone that lives in and improves the quality of soil

eight *n.*, a number whose value is greater than seven but less than nine

elephant *n.*, a large mammal with a long nose called a trunk and enormous ears

endangered *adj.*, in danger of becoming extinct

environment *n.*, everything that surrounds and affects an organism

equals *n.*, a symbol that indicates the result of a math operation

eraser *n.*, a school supply used to correct or eliminate mistakes made with a pencil

executive branch *n.*, the branch of the U.S. government that carries out the laws

exclamatory *adj.*, conveying excitement or volume

expanded notation *n.*, a form of writing a number showing the place value of its digits

experiment *n.*, a scientific way to test an idea

explained *v.*, made plain or understandable

explosives *n.*, items designed to burst loudly and violently

exports *n.*, the goods sent out of a country

extended family *adj.*, the members of a family who do not live with the parents and children in a household

exercise *n.*, the physical or mental activity done to improve health or to train for an event

extinct *adj.*, no longer living or in use

eyes *n.*, the parts of the body used for sight

F

fact family *n.*, a group of two additions and two subtractions that uses the same three numbers

family tree *n.*, a chart showing the relationship of all family members

famine *n.*, a drastic food shortage

fat *n.*, greasy or oily matter derived from animal tissue

federal government *n.*, an organized group with strong powers that makes laws for a country

feel *v.*, to experience; to touch; to believe

felt *v.*, past tense of the verb *to feel*

fields *n.,* large open areas of land used for growing crops

find *v.,* to locate or discover by searching

finishes *v.,* comes to an end or stops

flew *v.,* moved through the air

followed *v.,* went in the same direction

food groups *n.,* the categories of foods based on their nutritional properties

food guide pyramid *n.,* a graphic organizer that provides information for living a healthy lifestyle, including nutritional information and the importance of exercise

found *v.,* past tense of the verb *to find*

forests *n.,* thick growths of trees

fox *n.,* a small animal in the canine family

fraction *n.,* a part of a whole

freckles *n.,* small brownish spots on the skin

Friday *n.,* the last school day of a typical week

friends *n.,* the people you know, like, and trust

full moon *n.,* the phase of the moon when it is fully visible

fruit *n.,* the usually sweet part of a plant that can be eaten, such as bananas and cantaloupes

funny *adj.,* causing amusement or laughter

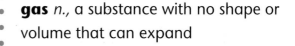

gas *n.,* a substance with no shape or volume that can expand

global positioning system *n.,* a device that uses satellites to track locations, usually referred to by its abbreviation (GPS)

glossary *n.,* an alphabetical list of words and their definitions that appears in the back of a book

go *v.,* to move or travel

gold mine *n.,* a place where gold is found in the earth

goods *n.,* merchandise or articles to be bought or sold

grains *n.,* seeds or fruits of various food plants, including those used to make pasta and bread

grandparents *n.,* the parents of one's mother or father

gravity *n.,* the natural force of attraction between masses

gray *adj.,* a color between black and white

Great Plains *n.,* a grassland area of central North America

gym *n.,* a school location where students meet with a teacher for physical education

——————— H ———————

habitat *n.,* the natural environment of an organism

half *n.,* one of two parts of a whole

happened *v.,* came upon something by chance

Haruko *n.,* girl in Amir's school who is from Japan

harvest *n.,* the food collected from fields at the end of a growing season

he *n.,* pronoun that stands for a male person or animal

heading *n.,* something at the top or beginning of a letter or other piece of writing

hear *v.,* to pay attention to or listen to

heat *n.,* a form of energy that causes a rise in temperature

height *n.,* the distance from the bottom to the top of something

help *v.,* to aid or give assistance

here *adv.,* in this place

hero *n.,* a person admired for his or her particular achievements or qualities

high *adj.,* of great altitude

hissing *n.,* a noise made by a thin but steady flow of air

history *n.,* a record of past events

Hopi *n.,* a Native American tribe that lives in Pueblos in northwest Arizona

how-to *adj.,* providing basic directions and instructions

human messengers *n.,* people who transport messages from town to town

hypothesis *n.,* a prediction of the outcome of a scientific experiment, which is tested to be proved or disproved

——————— I ———————

I'll *v.,* contraction of *I will*

I'm *v.,* contraction of *I am*

imagine *v.,* to form a mental picture of something

immigrants *n.,* the people who come to live in a new country

imperative *adj.,* unavoidable or absolutely necessary

imports *n.,* the goods brought in or transported from another country

impossible *adj.,* unable to be; not possible

inanimate *adj.,* lifeless; unmoving

indent *v.,* to begin a set distance in from a margin

index *n.*, an alphabetical list of topics in a book

insects *n.*, small animals with three sets of legs, a body, a head, and usually two sets of wings, such as butterflies, bees, and crickets

interrogative *adj.*, intended to elicit a response; asking a question

invertebrates *n.*, animals that do not have a backbone

island *n.*, a piece of land surrounded by water on all sides

it's *v.*, contraction of *it is*

— J —

Japan *n.*, the name of a country in Asia whose capital is Tokyo

judicial branch *n.*, the court system of the U.S. government

— K —

kilometer *n.*, unit of length equal to one thousand meters

knew *v.*, understood or grasped

knives *n.*, sharp cutting instruments with a blade and a handle

knows *v.*, understands or grasps

— L —

lake *n.*, a large body of fresh or salt water surrounded by land on all sides

landmarks *n.*, fixed markers or structures that serve to identify a location

lantern *n.*, a light that is carried in a protective case

late *adv.*, coming or being after the usual time

lb *n.*, abbreviation of *pound*

leaves *n.*, structures attached to plants and trees that are usually green

left *v.*, went out or away from

length *n.*, the measurement of something from end to end

let's *v.*, the contraction of *let us*

librarian *n.*, a person who works in a library

library *n.*, a place that contains books, magazines, and reference materials

life cycle *n.*, the stages of a living thing

lifestyle *n.*, the way in which a person or group lives

light *n.*, illumination from a light source, such as the sun or a lamp

lighthouse *n.*, a tall building with a strong light on top to guide ships and boats in bad weather

likes *v.*, takes pleasure in; enjoys

liquid *n.*, a fluid with no shape

list *n.*, a series of items written together in a group

lived *v.,* existed or was alive

lives *v.,* exists or is alive

local *adj.,* serving the needs of a particular place

long *adj.,* for en extended time or distance; tall

looked *v.,* used one's sight to view something or someone

loudly *adv.,* with relatively high volume

loves *v.,* has a deep feeling of affection

lunch bag *n.,* a paper container used to hold a light midday meal

────────── Ⓜ ──────────

made *v.,* produced by making

mail *v.,* to send by mail

main entrance *n.,* the primary entrance to a building

main office *n.,* a school location where secretaries and administrators conduct school business

map *n.,* a picture that shows the location of places or things

mast *n.,* a part of a sailboat that holds the sail

matter *n.,* anything that takes up space

mayor *n.,* the head of government in a town, city, or village

meat *n.,* flesh of animals used for food

met *v.,* came together; was introduced

meter *n.,* a unit of length equal to 39.37 inches

metric system *n.,* the decimal system of weights and measures

microscope *n.,* a scientific tool used to see tiny objects very close

millimeter *n.,* one thousandth of a meter

minerals *n.,* solid natural substances that are not plants or animals

minus *n.,* the symbol that indicates one number is being subtracted from another (–)

mirrors *n.,* objects that reflect the image of what is in front of them

mole *n.,* a small animal that lives underground and digs holes with his feet

Monday *n.,* the first school day after a weekend

money *n.,* bills and coins issued by a government for use as money

monsoon *n.,* a seasonal wind in southern Asia that brings heavy rainfalls

month *n.,* one of the twelve parts of a year; usually thirty or thirty-one days

moon *n.,* natural body that revolves around a planet

moonlight *n.,* illumination of the sun reflected off the moon onto Earth

most *adj.,* the greatest amount

mountain *n.,* a natural landform with an elevation higher than a hill

moved *v.,* changed position

multiplication *n.,* the process of adding a number to itself a certain number of times

museums *n.,* places where art or other objects are displayed for public view

— N —

Native Americans *n.,* the relatives of the original people who lived in North and South America before white settlers

natural resource *n.,* a usable stock or supply formed by nature

need *n.,* a requirement or necessity

nephew *n.,* the son of a person's brother or sister

never *adv.,* not ever; at no time

new moon *n.,* the moon's phase when it passes between the sun and Earth and appears invisible

nickel *n.,* a U.S. coin worth five cents

niece *n.,* the daughter of a person's brother or sister

nomads *n.,* people with no home who move from place to place

nonrenewable *adj.,* not able to be renewed

nose *n.,* the part of the body used for smelling and for breathing.

notebook *n.,* a school supply used to write in and organize notes

noun *n.,* a word that identifies a person, a place, or a thing

nutrition *n.,* the processes by which an animal or plant takes in and makes use of food

— O —

observations *n.,* what a scientist makes and records while testing an idea

often *adv.,* many times; frequently

oil *n.,* the liquids or substances that can become liquids when warmed, derived from greasy mineral, vegetable, human-made, or animal fats.

older *adj.,* advanced in years

opened *v.,* drew apart or separated

or *conj.,* as an alternative

orbits *v.,* revolves around

organism *n.,* an individual living being

ounce *n.,* a standard unit of measurement for liquids

owl *n.,* a nocturnal bird of prey with a broad head, very large eyes, a hooked beak, and strong claws

owned *v.,* had or possessed

oz *n.,* abbreviation of *ounce*

—————————— **P** ——————————

painted *v.,* covered with a coat of paint

paragraph *n.,* a group of sentences about one main idea

parents *n.,* father and mother

patrol car *n.,* police vehicle

pencil case *n.,* a school supply used to hold and organize pencils and other school supplies

peninsula *n.,* land surrounded by water on three sides

penny *n.,* a U.S. coin worth one cent

perimeter *n.,* the length around the outside of a shape

period *n.,* punctuation mark at the end of a declarative sentence

perspective *n.,* the use of lines to make objects in art appear closer or farther away

pesticides *n.,* chemicals used to kill pests such as insects

phases *n.,* stages of time or duration

picnic table *n.,* a piece of outdoor furniture upon which food is served and eaten

plaid *n.,* a pattern of unevenly spaced, repeated stripes crossing at right angles

plain *n.,* a large, flat area usually without trees

place value *n.,* the value of a digit according to its place in a number

planet *n.,* celestial body that circles the sun

plate *n.,* a shallow or flat dish off which food is eaten

playground *n.,* an outdoor school location where students go to play at recess

plow *v.,* a farm machine used to break up soil before planting

plural *adj.,* relating to a word that represents more than one

plus *n.,* a symbol that indicates one number amount is being combined with another (+)

police detective *n.,* a police officer who investigates crimes

pollution *n.,* something that pollutes or adds harmful substances to the environment

polygon *n.,* a closed figure that has three or more straight sides

pond *n.,* a body of water that is smaller than a lake

pound *n.,* the standard unit of weight equal to sixteen ounces

principal *n.,* a school worker who runs the school and works mostly in an office

preposition *n.,* a word that describes relationships between two or more nouns or pronouns

principal's office *n.,* the room where a principal works

president *n.,* the chief executive or leader of a country

product *n.,* the result of a multiplication operation

proper nouns *n.,* capitalized nouns that are specific names of people, places, or things

pronoun *n.,* a word that stands in the place of a noun or noun phrase

properties *n.,* characteristic traits

Pueblo *n.,* Native American peoples who live in pueblo villages in New Mexico and Arizona

quarter *n.,* a U.S. coin worth twenty-five cents; one of four equal parts

quickly *adv.,* with speed; rapidly

quietly *adv.,* with low volume

quotient *n.,* the result of a division operation

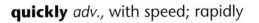

radar *n.,* an electronic device used to determine location or speed

railroads *n.,* systems of railroad tracks, stations, and trains used for transportation

recipe *n.,* set of instructions to prepare something, such as food

recycling *v.,* collecting and processing used or abandoned materials to make new products

red *adj.,* any of the various colors resembling blood or a ruby

remainder *n.,* the number left over when one number is divided by another

renewable *adj.,* able to be renewed

reporter *n.,* a person hired to report news

rescue *v.,* to save or set free

reservations *n.,* pieces of land set apart by the U.S. government for Native Americans to live on

resources *n.* available supplies that can be used as needed

restart *v.,* to start again

ride *v.,* to travel or be transported

river *n.,* a large natural stream of water that flows into another body of water

rocks *n.,* pieces or fragments of stone

row *v.,* to move through water by using an oar

ruler *n.,* a school supply used to measure the lengths of objects

rumble *n.,* a deep, long sound

said *v.,* expressed in words

sailboat *n.,* a boat that uses the power of the wind, caught in sails, to move

sandwich *n.,* two or more slices of bread with a filling in between

satellite *n.,* a body of land or other large object that revolves around, or orbits, a planet

salutation *n.,* a greeting usually followed by the name of the person you are writing or speaking to

Saturday *n.,* the first day of the weekend

saved *v.,* rescued from danger

saw *v.,* looked at; observed

school nurse *n.,* a school worker who helps students with illnesses or injuries

season *n.,* one of four parts of a year with characteristic weather patterns

senses *n.,* faculties of sight, smell, hearing, taste, and touch

sentence *n.,* a group of words that expresses a complete thought

serious *adj.,* of or showing deep thought

she *n.,* a pronoun that stands in for a female person or animal

shelter *n.,* something that provides cover or protection

shirt *n.,* long- or short-sleeved garment for the upper part of the body

shop *v.,* to visit stores to purchase items

short *adj.,* having little length or height; not long

shorts *n.,* trousers that are knee length or shorter

shoulder *n.,* the part of the human body between the neck and the upper arm

siblings *n.,* brothers or sisters

signature *n.,* a person's name as written by that person

single parent *n.,* a mother or father who brings up a child or children on his or her own

singular *adj.,* relating to a word that represents one person, place, or thing

skies *n.,* areas above the earth

skirt *n.,* a one-piece garment that hangs from the waist and is not joined at the legs

smoke signals *n.,* messages transmitted over distances by sending up puffs of smoke from a fire

soccer ball *n.*, an inflated ball used for the sport of soccer

so *conj.*, for that reason

soils *n.*, certain types of earth or ground at the top of Earth's surface

solar energy *n.*, energy from the sun

solar system *n.*, the sun planets, stars, and other bodies in the sky

solid *n.*, a substance with shape and volume

Southwest *n.*, an area of the United States that includes Arizona, California, Colorado, Nevada, New Mexico, and Utah

sometimes *adv.*, on some occasions

special lenses *n.*, specific clear materials used for viewing

sphere *n.*, a solid geometric shape that is round

spike *n.*, a thin, sharp, long piece of metal or wood

splashes *v.*, scatters liquids

spring *n.*, season between winter and summer

standard notation *n.*, written form of numbers using 0–9

stars *n.*, large spheres of hot gas that usually appear in the night sky as twinkling lights

starts *v.*, begins a movement or activity

state *n.*, the condition of matter

state-of-being verb *n.*, a word that tells about the condition, location, or origin of someone or something

steps *n.*, a series of actions to achieve a goal; stages in a process

still life *n.*, a painting of inanimate objects

stopped *v.*, put an end to

storm *n.*, a weather condition with strong winds and precipitation

stretched *v.*, extended to full length

strict *adj.*, enforcing rules

subject *n.*, the noun or pronoun in a sentence that is the doer of the action of the verb

subtraction *n.*, math operation indicated by a minus sign (–)

sum *n.*, result of an addition operation

Sunday *n.*, the last day of the weekend, before most people return to work or school

sunlight *n.*, the light of the sun

supply *n.*, an amount of something available for a specific use

support *v.*, to uphold, defend, or help

T

table of contents *n.*, a list of the chapters or units in a book and the page numbers where each begins

talked *v.*, expressed orally in words

tall *adj.*, having relatively great height

talons *n.*, sharp, curved claws on birds

teacher *n.*, a school worker who provides students with instruction and homework

technology *n.*, systems for the development of electronic or digital products

teepees *n.*, the cone-shaped homes of certain Native Americans made with poles covered by animal skins

telegram *n.*, a message sent by telegraph

telegraph *n.*, a communication system to send messages through electronic pulses

telegraph lines *n.*, a system of wires that connect telegraph systems

telephone *n.*, a communication device that carries voice waves over electrical wires

telescope *n.*, a device that uses lenses to help a person see a distant object as if it was close

theater *n.*, a building for dramatic presentations, shows, or movies

they *n.*, a plural pronoun for he, she, and it

thief *n.*, person or animal that steals

thin *adj.*, of less than average width

third *n.*, one of three equal parts

Thursday *n.*, the day that comes after Wednesday

tide *n.*, the regular rise and fall of water in oceans, bays, and seas

times *n.*, occurrences or replications

title page *n.*, the first page of a book that lists the title, author's name, publisher, and the city where it was published

Tino *n.*, a boy from Amir's school who is from the Dominican Republic

tongue *n.*, the part of the body found in the mouth, used for taste, swallowing, chewing, and speech

too *adv.*, also; in addition

took *v.*, obtained or gained possession of

topic sentence *n.*, a sentence that states the main idea of a paragraph

torn down *v.*, pulled apart or destroyed

tower *n*, a building that is very tall but not very wide

town hall *n.*, building used for a town's business; also *city hall*

traditional *adj.*, of or pertaining to tradition

traffic *n.,* the movement of vehicles along streets, roads or other transportation areas

train station *n.,* a place where trains load and unload passengers or goods

traits *n.,* distinguishing characteristics

transport *v.,* to carry from one place to another

tray *n.,* a flat container with edges used to carry things

treasure hunt *n.,* a game in which players try to find hidden objects by solving a series of clues

tried *v.,* attempted to do

T-shirts *n.,* short-sleeved, collarless shirts

Tuesday *n.,* the day between Monday and Wednesday

tunnels *n.,* underground passages

two *n.,* number equal to one plus one

— U —

uncles *n.,* the brothers of one's mother or father

unable *adj.,* incapable or not able

unusual *adj.,* not usual or common

use *v.,* to make use of

usually *adv.,* under normal conditions

— V —

valley *n.,* a large area of land surrounded by mountains

vegetables *n.,* the parts of plants that can be eaten, such as spinach, broccoli, and carrots

verbs *n.,* words that express the actions of a subject

verb *to be* *n.,* a word that is used to express a state of being

vertebrates *n.,* animals that have a backbone or spinal column

veterans *n.,* persons who served in the military

— W —

wagons *n.,* vehicles with four wheels usually pulled by horses

waited *v.,* remained or was in readiness for something or someone

walk *v.,* to travel on foot

want *n.,* something wished for or desired

wanted *v.,* wished for or desired

warm-blooded *adj.,* having a set body temperature independent of the environment's temperature

was *v.,* existed or lived

Wednesday *n.,* the day between Tuesday and Thursday

weight *n.,* the measure of how heavy an object or being is

went *v.,* moved to or from something

we're *v.,* contraction of *we are*

were *v.,* existed or lived

wetlands *n.,* areas that have wet soil and vegetation such as swamps

whale oil *n.,* a fat made from whale blubber

whole *n.,* a complete thing, such as a number or set

wide *adj.,* having great length from side to side

width *n.,* length from side to side

will be *v.,* about to be; going to be

will do *v.,* about to do; going to do

will feel *v.,* about to feel; going to feel

will give *v.,* about to give; going to give

will listen *v.,* about to listen or going to listen

will make *v.,* about to make; going to make

will stay *v.,* about to stay; going to stay

will take *v.,* about to take; going to take

will work *v.,* about to work; going to work

wolves *n.,* animals in the canine family that live in packs

won't *v.,* contraction of *will not*

──────────── Y ────────────

younger *adj.,* in an earlier period of life or development